Internet in Education

Internet in Education

Integrating the Internet into the TESOL Classroom

David Kent

National Library of Australia Cataloguing-in-Publication entry:
Kent, David Bradley, author.
Internet in Education : Integrating the Internet into the TESOL Classroom / David Kent.

ISBN: 9781925555158 (paperback)
Includes bibliographical references.
Teachers of English to Speakers of Other Languages.
Internet in education—Study and teaching.
Teaching—Aids and devices.
Educational technology.
English language—Study and teaching—Foreign speakers.

Pedagogy Press. Sydney, Australia.
www.pedagogypress.com

First Edition.

DEDICATION

For the four.

CONTENTS

ACKNOWLEDGMENTS

I wish to extend my deepest appreciation to my wife *Hyunhee* who has been very patient and understanding throughout the entire process involved with the writing and producing of this book. I would also like to thank *Noel David* for his suggestions and patience. This book would not have been written without him.

PREFACE

Technological advancement is rapid, and its impact on teaching and learning is ever constant. This leads to a need for educators to continually assess and consider the implication that new and emerging technologies may hold for their teaching context, their professional development, and the skills possessed and required by their students. This is where the value of this book becomes apparent, as practitioners will be able to walk away with a greater understanding of how to best employ various aspects of technology-driven learning, instruction, and assessment techniques when teaching English to speakers of other languages (TESOL) from a variety of pedagogical contexts.

1. Introduction

1. Introduction

In a world where there is still a digital divide (Mossberger, Tolbert & Stansbury, 2003), and where many second-language learners are digital natives (Prensky, 2001), the internet has unquestionably come to provide significant impact on the way that we communicate, teach, learn, and live. Consisting of millions of interconnected devices, it plays increasingly important roles in the educational life of learners around the globe by providing knowledge-on-demand for just-in-time learning, and offers great potential for providing diversified learning opportunities in the classroom context when conducting the teaching of English to speakers of other languages (TESOL).

The major pedagogical promise emerging from the internet for second-language learners has come with the shift from that of Web 1.0, a static internet providing information to users, to that of Web 2.0, an internet that allows for dynamic information sharing. This has led to the emergence of user-generated content (UGC), changes in the ways that we access this content, and changes in the ways we conduct synchronous and asynchronous computer-mediated communication. The internet has become much more than a source of authentic materials and supplemental resources; it now provides a means for students to engage in functional communicative experiences, write and communicate with a wider audience, and showcase their work. All kinds of topics and resources are available, but most websites and applications prove unsuitable in supporting language learning, and most require the need for guidance to be effective, and it is here where the teacher and this book performs a critical role. Resources need to be selected wisely, and students need to be guided in their use to keep those with little experience in using digital tools and websites for learning from experiencing anxiety or becoming disengaged. Importantly too, any use of online-dependent technology requires a contingency plan in case something goes wrong with the hardware or applications being used.

Nonetheless, the internet does brings with it learning opportunities that are increasingly interactive, social, and multimodal (Richards, 2014). This, of course, has also seen changes in the ways that instructors must teach, provide, and assess content, interact with their students, engage with resources, and develop their craft. Examples here include: flipping the classroom; applying bring-your-own-device (BYOD); integrating app use and normalizing technological use; working with digital textbooks and digitizing story times; developing increasingly visual- and multimedia-focused presentations; engaging in computer-mediated communication (CMC) by constructing visually-based digital conversations both synchronously and asynchronously; providing online tutoring; emailing reports; relying on just-in-time downloads for classroom activities; developing data-driven learning by engaging in aspects of concordancing and vocab profiling; becoming increasingly exposed to social media and cloud-based learning and teaching techniques; and coping with the gamification of learning and the student need for coding skills – all this while developing online virtual personal learning environments (PLEs). Along with these changes has also come the rise and reliance on social media, accompanied by an ever-increasing use of technology to assist learners with their language skill development.

Organization of the Book

Internet in Education aims to cover the use and applicability of various technologies and applications specifically for instructors who are teaching English to speakers of other languages (TESOL) in English as a foreign language (EFL) environments, and it is also worthwhile to any English as a second language (ESL) teacher. In this book, subtitled *Integrating the Internet into the TESOL Classroom,* the focus is on the use of various tools and techniques that help students to express themselves and to learn with technology, particularly those which rely on the internet to function, those that have been around since the dawn of the internet, and those that have evolved with the growth of the internet.

The book is intended to be read as a whole or in part by teachers, students, parents, and any other stakeholders who may be interested in the topics. Each chapter follows a similar layout, and begins with a short overview in order to situate topics. The overview is followed by a discussion of the relevance of the topic to the wider context of education, prior to presenting the aspects that make that topic effective. How the topic can best be applied in the teaching of English to speakers of other languages (TESOL) context is then introduced, along with a means to evaluate any learner-developed content that may result. Methods for developing effective implementation of the topic are then explored at length before finalizing the chapter with key points. In line with this, each chapter focuses on a single technology topic, and is designed around a question-based format, similar to that outlined here:

- Overview
- What is … ?
- How can I use … ?
- What types of … exist?
- What elements are behind an effective … ?
- How can … lend itself to TESOL?
- How can I start using … with students?
- How do I evaluate a … ?
- What tools are available for … creation?
- How do I craft a … ?
- How would I use a tool to create a … ?
- What are the key points behind … use in the TESOL context?

Chapter One provides the rationale for today's teachers' need of the book, and it lays out the organization of the text. *Chapter Two* examines the WebQuest model in light of the emergence of Web 2.0, and takes into account teacher-directed but student-centered world-wide-web utilization for the fostering and development of multiple literacies, with focus placed on the socio-constructivist learning theory behind the model, and how this is applicable to the second-language learner. *Chapter Three* presents the use of an interactive tool that allows for collaboration, sharing, and commenting, and is one that can provide a voice to all students in the classroom as they construct visually-based asynchronous digital conversations. How this changes the ways that information can be presented, disseminated, and discussed online is provided, while illustrating the efficacy and pedagogical affordances of using VoiceThread. *Chapter Four* provides a means of engaging learners with content using social media platforms in the form of blogs and wikis to develop user-generated content that demands interaction.

Lesson plan guides, example implementation techniques, and various free-to-use handouts for both instructors and their students are included in *Chapters Five and Six*. A comprehensive list of resources, with links to pertinent web sites and applications, can be found in *Chapter Seven*. A reference list of all works cited is given in *Chapter Eight*, and it allows teachers to engage in further reading on the issues that most interest them and impact their students.

It is hoped that this book will provide both education and something new for all teachers – be they trained or untrained, pre-service, in-service, seasoned, or retired.

2. World-Wide-Web utilization: WebQuests

2. World-Wide Web utilization: WebQuests

Overview

This chapter focuses on the use and applicability of WebQuests in the 21st century educational environment, particularly as they relate to the teaching of English to speakers of other languages (TESOL). With the need to develop and foster multiple literacies in our students today, the WebQuest model is as relevant now as it was at the dawn of the internet. To this end, aspects of the model best suited to the TESOL context are provided, with the learning theory behind the development of the WebQuest model covered in detail. The types of WebQuests that are available and the topics best suited to WebQuest creation are also covered, along with effective development techniques, the types of WebQuests, and the benefits and adaptability of using the model with TESOL students is explored. This is augmented by the provision of various evaluation strategies for assessing self-created and pre-developed WebQuests, and for assessing any WebQuest that students may complete during class. The tools and templates to develop a WebQuest for classroom use are then highlighted, with a practitioner guide to this process arising from the included material that is useable as classroom content, with a number of photocopiable handouts that go along with it. This is further supported by a wide variety of additional resources to assist in the use and development of WebQuests for the classroom.

What is a WebQuest?

Dr. Bernie Dodge, as professor of Educational Technology at San Diego State University, is the originator of the WebQuest model which was developed in the mid-1990s with contributions from Tom March, Educational Technology staff of the San Diego Unified School District (Dodge, 2015). Since that time, and with the growth of the internet, many teachers have been able to employ this model, developing their own WebQuests that they used with their students, and then made freely available for other educators to download.

Like the models used to develop lesson plans, the WebQuest model, although now over two decades old, still holds its own as an inquiry-oriented learning tool. As opposed to the 'traditional' model of learning, relying on mastery of skills and an empty vessel approach with a 'sage on the stage', inquiry-oriented learning focuses more on using and learning content in order to develop skills such as problem-solving or information processing. Inquiry-based learning, combined with technology models in the EFL context, has led to an improvement in student linguistic skills, increased the development of social skills, the learning of different cultural aspects, and to gains in wider perspectives on topics (Arauz, 2013).

Ultimately, there are five distinguishing characteristics of a WebQuest (EBC, 2004). First, Webquests are classroom-based lessons where all or most of the information that students explore and evaluate comes from the internet. Second, emphasis is placed on the development of analysis, promotion of creativity, criticism, and other higher-order thinking skills, over that of simply information gathering. Third, as all of the internet sources are teacher-selected and -presented, the tasks are heavily teacher-guided but remain student-centered with an emphasis on information use. Fourth, students are intended to take on various roles as part of a WebQuest. And fifth, WebQuests are usually group-oriented.

As such, WebQuests offer the following to students of instructors that are Teaching English to Speakers of Other Languages (TESOL):

- A means to utilize all that the internet has to offer, but in a controlled manner.
- Present teacher-directed and -developed content that leads to intensively student-focused lessons.
- Provide teaching material that promotes learner autonomy by requiring students to use, rely on, and develop their own skills as they work through the presented learning content together.
- Ensure that learners gain access to authentic language and learning content from within a technology-rich framework.

Establish a learning environment where students can begin to focus on using language collaboratively to process information as well as engage in problem solving activities.

How can I use WebQuests?

WebQuests are classroom-based lessons where all or most of the information that students explore and evaluate is internet-based. They emphasize higher-order thinking, and are teacher-guided but student-centered, with information use and understanding developed from role-based involvement with learning content that enables students to then work out a conclusion or answer to the set task(s) or problem(s). These lessons are classroom-based and each can be incorporated into a 50-minute single lesson used as a once-off, developed for use as part of a month long unit, or incorporated into the curriculum for an entire semester. WebQuests can be used to promote learning and motivation while employing constructivism, situated learning, and inquiry-based learning principles.

The key behind the successful development and use of a WebQuest is to use the internet to provide motivating learning material in the form of an authentic task, and present this material to students using a scaffolded learning approach which is based on constructivism and situated learning that they must then take on board to complete by taking on roles and participating in an inquiry-based method of learning (March, 2004).

Motivating Tasks

From the outset, any WebQuest task needs to be designed to motivate learners to want to learn or begin a quest of discovery using the materials and roles provided by the WebQuest itself. Tasks need to be built upon internet-based material that provides some level of interactivity, are media dense, contain different perspectives, and are tailored to the teaching and learning context of students. In this way, WebQuests can begin to offer more than textbooks, photocopiable handouts, or activity-based worksheets, and provide motivation for learners to engage with the content and to begin to challenge their own perspectives.

Tasks therefore rely on authentic content to be completed successfully, and lead students to develop knowledge and participate in learning through contextualization based on a socio-constructivist model of scaffolded learning.

Scaffolding

Scaffolding can be built into a good WebQuest by providing partly completed tasks, and by finding the best resources for participants to work out how to complete them. Learners then use this content to form their background understanding, or build upon existing schema, before they begin to engage with more specific resources targeting their specialized role in the WebQuest. Scaffolding thereby provides learners with the opportunity to contextualize content knowledge and engage in situated learning (Pederson, 2013; Chou, 2014). This method allows for teachers to think about teaching differently. WebQuests provide a means for the teacher to move from being a 'sage on the stage' to a 'guide on the side' during lesson time, and even though the content and material is extremely teacher-provided, the activities are student–centered. Learners engage with the material and employ the content during class time to build their own knowledge and develop their own personal meanings and understandings of the content before coming together to make sense of it. It is this deep understanding, developed from scaffolded knowledge, that is then presented to the teacher for evaluation. In order to do this successfully, students must provide each other with assistance to socially negotiate meaning. They can do this by exchanging resources with each other, and by offering each other feedback. It is also in this way that individuals can be held accountable for their own learning, as well as the learning development of others.

Questioning

Any question that can be answered 'yes' or 'no', or is able to be answered by cutting and pasting, is not suitable for inclusion in a good WebQuest. Questions must be those that students can answer directly via investigation or by engaging in inquiry. Good WebQuest questions are also those that take into account students current academic and language skill levels, as well as the relevant prior knowledge that might be required of the WebQuest overall.

The questions must promote critical thinking skills. In other words, questions must ensure that students need to do more than participate in information gathering activities. Students should be able to examine the information collated, and process it to form their own opinions about the topic or subject matter. WebQuests primarily achieve this by assigning specific roles to individuals or specific group members, and therefore these individuals or groups then have their own research agenda to carry out, and this must then be discussed and presented to all group members to resolve the overall problem, situation, or task presented as the main WebQuest end goal.

Answers must not be already known
"What is K-pop?" is a little too straightforward for a WebQuest. "What musical styles does K-Pop draw from, and how is this represented on stage and in music videos?" offers a much wider opportunity for research and exploration.

Answers must not be simple facts
"In what year did the Korean War start?" can be looked up very easily online, can be asked of a friend or relative, or may already be known. "What factors led to the start of the Korean War?" is a better question, as it requires research, interpretation, and analysis.

Answers should not be too personal
"Why do you like K-Pop?" can lead to internalization and to thinking about the self. "What have people said about K-Pop recently?" would see students research the question based on gender, or other demographics such as age.

Answers must contain an objective basis

"Does long term sun exposure cause skin cancer?" calls for a value judgment, whereas "What does the evidence suggest is the cause of skin cancer?" calls for research.

Answers must be answerable

"What factors have led the song *arirang* to become representative of Korea?" is answerable, perhaps many ways, whereas "Why was the fourth word of the second line of the song *arirang* chosen by the composer?" could not be answered with any certainty.

Ultimately, WebQuests can be used in the classroom for knowledge acquisition and integration, as well as extending and defining the depth of student knowledge. As such, WebQuests can be used to close off a topic as a review piece in the short-term. They can also lead into longer-term portfolio pieces to be used for grading and for demonstrations of meeting standards, and to provide take-home material for stakeholders such as parents, administration, and even the learners themselves. This leads us into the two types of WebQuests.

What are the two types of WebQuest?

The two types of WebQuest are short-term and long-term, and each has its own goal.

Type One – The short-term WebQuest

The goal of the short-term WebQuest is knowledge acquisition and integration where the learner engages with a significant amount of new information, and comes to make sense of it. The short-term WebQuest would only ever cover one to three class periods. It is useful to consolidate skills, such as a need to develop a booktrailer based on a class assigned novel after completing a digital storytelling unit.

Other good examples of short-term WebQuests involve students working in teams that require them to take on immediate roles to solve a problem, such as determining the reasons behind the death of a King or the substantiation of the rumor that Mozart was murdered by a rival composer (Benjamin, 2003).

Type Two – The long-term WebQuest

The goal of the long-term WebQuest is to extend and define knowledge. The learner is expected to deeply analyze the body of available knowledge, and create something to which others can respond. The long-term WebQuest might cover from one week to one month of class time, and it also provides an opportunity to create portfolio projects and the assessment of group skills longitudinally, while simultaneously being able to provide a demonstrable outcome that can be shared with other stakeholders (such as student peers, parents, and administration).

The challenge with a long-term WebQuest is that it needs to sustain student interest. Such WebQuests will also typically need to meet several standards if used in a school setting, and might therefore need to include interdisciplinary work. An example might be to create an itinerary for a family group visiting Korea where investigation of the people, climate, economy, culture, customs, available leisure activities, cuisine, and the physical geography of the nation are all likely to be taken into account. Investigating each of these areas supports a broad range of disciplines (for example, history, geography, sports, mathematics, and culinary arts). Multi-literacies are also supported when gathering country specific information from different kinds of text (for example, books, articles, and brochures) and interpreting data when listening to and watching various media types (for example, documentaries on the one hand and contemporary music videos on the other). Digital literacies are further addressed when using technology as a means to cohesively tie the information together.

Whatever the length of the WebQuest, the ultimate goal is to see learners enjoy the undertaking and participation in projects, and to ultimately help develop within them aspects of learner autonomy and the ability to undertake research. This is achieved particularly when students actively engage in group discussions when exploring a central issue, and develop the necessary searching and critical thinking skills to examine the information sources that are presented to them. For second-language learners, the opportunity for linguistic development also arises when they use the target language for reading information, listening to audio materials, and watching videos relating to the WebQuest topic, then writing presentations and listening to peers' opinions and ideas when discussing the critical issues that relate to the topic and the final outcome of the WebQuest.

What elements are behind an effective WebQuest layout?

There is a set WebQuest format which serves well as a guide to follow when beginning to construct a WebQuest for students (EBC, 2004). Becoming familiar with this layout will also help in thinking through some of the key elements behind WebQuest development when it comes time to develop one of your own, or assessing the use of one designed by another teacher for use with your students.

The layout involves an introduction or description, statement of the task itself, the process required to complete the task, resources required while engaging in the process, the evaluation method used by the teacher, and a means of conclusion or presentation of the completed task.

Introduction

Establish clear and concise background information, learning goals, and motivational scenarios that engage students (for example, "You are an astronaut going to the moon."). Include the reasons why the topic is one worthy of investigating.

Task

Set an interesting and concrete central task, and provide a formal description of what students will have accomplished by the end of the WebQuest. The task is the focus for the learners' activities, so consider those that are motivating, inspirational, and potentially fun to engage in.

Process

This is the section of the WebQuest where you provide a description of all the steps that learners should go through in order to accomplish the task. The roles of each group member need to be made very clear in this step. Include guidance and support, and potentially tips on how to divide responsibilities amongst students, or how to find and organize the information or resources that will be collated for analysis. Any description of roles and responsibilities should be offered together with scaffolding tools (like handouts and templates).

Resources

Resources are all the items that students will need to complete the task, and include bookmarked websites, print resources, and online multimedia sources. Resources can also extend to include non-web-based content such as audio/video as well as field trips to locations such as museums. This can be a separate section, or the resources can be presented on an as-needed basis throughout the 'Process' section. It is now encouraged by Dodge (2016) to include the necessary elements from the resources section in the process section as they are required in a fully developed and completed WebQuest. However, in the early developmental stages of a WebQuest when it is being created by a teacher, it may prove easier to keep these sections separated so that each section of the layout has a single process that needs focusing upon at the time it is being written up. Essentially, as WebQuests provide all relevant links to students as they are designed to extremely efficient and focused lessons that can prevent students from wandering around the internet and going off-task. All material should be pre-selected by the teacher.

Evaluation

Each WebQuest needs an evaluation rubric, with fair, clear, consistent, and specific components relative to the tasks set. Further details on development and inclusion of a rubric for WebQuest assessment are discussed later in this book.

Conclusion

There are two elements of this section: reflection by students, and a summary of the goals and achievements provided by completing the WebQuest presented by the teacher. Time should also be set aside to discuss any potential points of interest or elements of application emerging from the student reflection session. Typical final projects presented in conclusion might consist of oral presentations as well as presentations based on written materials (for example, brochure development, newsletter creation, or blog and wiki development).

How do WebQuests lend themselves to TESOL?

WebQuests offer several benefits to second-language learners of English, including:

1. They provide exposure to a significant amount of authentic language, primarily when engaging in the reading of texts for task completion, but also when processing any included streaming media (audio- or video-based).

2. They develop co-operation skills in students. Students who work together to complete tasks and roles can enhance their communicative opportunities and in turn their linguistic abilities through language practice.

3. They can encourage motivation and learner engagement. This is achieved if they are developed with an appropriate hook, and they appeal to students interests.

4. They provide support for several learning methods. Constructivist learning theory is supported through the use of scaffolding and learning from a zone of proximal development (ZPD). Students engage with the development of knowledge through a situational learning context driven by inquiry-based learning methods.

For WebQuests, focus is often placed on the reading of material for task and role completion, and in turn the writing up of this information for presentation. In the TESOL context in this regard, WebQuests have been used to support the development of reading and writing opportunities for students, especially for developing critical reading skills, with Ahmad (2012) seeing that WebQuests are useful for this purpose among college level students of English as a foreign language (EFL). Alshumaimeri and Almasri (2012) also view WebQuests as beneficial for developing the reading skills of students, particularly for increasing comprehension skills. However, they also warn that teachers and students need to be trained or fully understand how to go about delivering and conducting a WebQuest in order to gain full benefit from the use of this model.

Other benefits that have emerged for second-language learners using WebQuests see apprehension of writing reduced and writing performance enhanced (Chuo, 2007), while simultaneously providing authentic learning materials and collaborative tasks (Kocoglu, 2010). Zlatkovska (2010) also recognizes that WebQuests provide a more student-centered and constructivist model of teaching, which facilitates English language teaching and technology integration as part of non-native speaker English teacher training.

An important aspect to consider when using an existing WebQuest is its suitability for the TESOL context. In this regard, as Prapinwong and Puthikanon (2008) remind us, five factors are important to take into account, and these include the vocabulary and grammar levels of students, along with their prior knowledge, the interestingness provided by the WebQuest, and the amount of assistance/scaffolding provided to the learner to complete the tasks. Assessing the potential use or modification of a WebQuest is always important, as it is with any learning material developed by another teacher for use with your own students and teaching style.

What topics are suitable for WebQuests?

Webquests can be applied to a range of topics, but not all. The topics that they are most suitable for involve tasks that require creativity, and have problems with several possible solutions.

WebQuests can address open-ended questions like:
- What should be done to protect Australia's Great Barrier Reef?
- What can be done to save what's left of the Amazon rainforest?
- What was it like to live during the Australian gold rush?
- What was it like to live in Korea under Japanese colonial rule?

For students of a lower language level, like second-language learners and young learners, the following roles may be more appropriate.
- Book reviewer: working as a member of a team to develop a trailer for an upcoming book launch. This lends itself to any book, and any level of student.
- Reporter: working as a member of a team to produce a magazine section consisting of several articles. Topics of the section can be broad, and focus on travel, cuisine, or important cultural events.
- Investigator: working as a member of an elite police squad investigating all of the clues assigned to a particular role (beat detective, crime scene investigator, medical examiner) to solve a murder mystery.
- Travel agent: investigate the economy, leisure activities, accommodations, and cuisine of a certain

country or group of countries for a one month family
vacation and to be included in a travel brochure.

For the TESOL context overall, the tasks or roles set by the
WebQuest should encourage use of the target language. For
example, gathering information from written resources provides
learners with reading practice, after which, the information
acquired can be discussed in groups before then being put into
practice (by perhaps developing a brochure). Tasks should also
promote collaboration and meaningful communication amongst
students, with the material presented for use being not only
authentic but which they would likely use or come across in
their daily lives (Koenraad & Westhoff, 2003).

How do I evaluate WebQuests?

Perhaps the most appropriate means available to evaluate
pre-existing and self-created WebQuests, particularly for use in
the TESOL context, is to use a prefabricated rubric based upon a
Likert-type rating scale. Similar rubrics can also be applied to the
work that students produce after completing a WebQuest. In this
case, any such rubric should be presented to students
beforehand, so that they can understand what will be assessed
and expected from them.

Evaluation rubrics, particularly those using indicators across
several categories, are essential when assessing the quality of
WebQuests that are freely available for download, but even
those that are well-developed they may have been created for
slightly different teaching contexts than yours. While it is useful
for the busy teacher to apply pre-made rubrics it is even better if
teacher to formulate ones of their own that reflect their specific
teaching environment and the points that they wish to assess.

One good source for this is Rubistar, where there are a number of pre-made evaluation options as well as information on how to create unique context sensitive evaluation instruments. The rubrics section of the resources list also contains several other rubric creation tools that may prove worthwhile to look over.

The rating scale used in the following rubrics goes from 1 to 5, with 1 being poor, 2 fair, 3 average, 4 good, and 5 excellent. 'Average' is used as a midpoint so that students can see how each particular skill relates to peers. This allows teachers to identify those skills that are weak in individual students, and those that may need improvement.

Pre-Developed/Self-Created WebQuest

Assessment Item	Assessment Criteria	Score
Introduction	Relates to learner interests; describes a compelling question or problem.	1 2 3 4 5
Task	Engaging, and elicits thinking that goes beyond rote comprehension.	1 2 3 4 5
Processes	Different roles are assigned to help students share responsibility in accomplishing the task.	1 2 3 4 5
Resources	There is a clear and meaningful connection between resources and the required information.	1 2 3 4 5
Evaluation	The criteria for success are clear, with the evaluation instrument measuring what students must know and be able to do when the WebQuest is complete.	1 2 3 4 5

Ratings: 1 Poor 2 Fair 3 Average 4 Good 5 Excellent

Student Completed WebQuest

Assessment Item	Assessment Criteria	Score
Introduction	Questions answered completely, with clear and sound rationale behind the answers.	1 2 3 4 5
Task	The task is completed, and the means of completing the task, or the plan followed to achieve it, is well executed.	1 2 3 4 5
Processes	Students clearly worked well as a team, with the final product a result of equal collaboration amongst all members.	1 2 3 4 5
Resources	Ideas expressed are based on the resources provided, but demonstrate originality.	1 2 3 4 5
Evaluation and Conclusion	Students were able to achieve the final goal of the WebQuest, with the final presented work substantially free of language errors such as grammar and spelling, and with the expected formatting or presentation method followed.	1 2 3 4 5

Ratings: 1 Poor 2 Fair 3 Average 4 Good 5 Excellent

What tools are available for WebQuest creation?

There is no specific software tool available to develop a WebQuest. However, there are a number of templates available and a number of websites and applications that will use a software-based template and present a model to help you develop a WebQuest in the correct format. These websites can be found in the resources list, under WebQuest, and two template-driven sites are discussed in more detail a little later in this book.

The rudimentary template that is followed when creating a WebQuest has the following:
- Introduction – orients and captures interest
- Task – presents the required end goal
- Process – details steps to achieve the end goal
- Resources – provides materials for the task
- Evaluation – measures the results
- Conclusion – presents the results

Aspects of the above components need to be crafted by the individual teacher as they go. Keep in mind that WebQuests are designed to use student time efficiently, as students are using the links to resource material provided and are not out searching for it. When accessing such content, students also need to rely on higher order thinking skills (analysis, synthesis, and evaluation techniques) to engage with it effectively. As a result, Dodge (2001), has determined that *focus* is pivotal to the creation of a good WebQuest, that is: *f*inding excellent sites, *o*rchestrating learners and resources, *c*hallenging thinking in learners, *u*sing mediums to advantage, and *s*caffolding great expectations.

Finding excellent sites

Assess sites for authenticity to task, interestingness to students, relevancy for language learning, and for content that is up-to-date.

Orchestrating learners and resources

Establish tasks and processes that guide learners to be cooperative, collaborative, accountable, and reflect upon their work, and that require a need to share information between all members of the team so that only in this way can the task actually be accomplished.

Judiciously use and apply all the materials that you have access to from your teaching and learning context (both physical and virtually accessible); that is, develop offline and online lesson components to accommodate the teaching and learning context as necessary.

Challenging thinking in learners

Learner is no longer simply about the memorization of information and facts; students today need to be able to work in teams and collaborate on projects. Creativity and imagination needs to be developed alongside critical thinking and problem solving abilities, and these need to be incorporated into any classroom content that students engage with for learning and for communicating. Multi-literacy skills (including information literacy, media literacy, and technology literacy) are also increasingly being emphasized, along with social and cross-cultural skills, and traits leading to adaptability and flexibility, productivity and accountability, initiative and self-direction, as well as leadership and responsibility.

The task set by the WebQuest needs to accommodate the development of these skills and traits, and it is recognized that the task is the key component to successful WebQuest design. Tasks must go beyond retelling, and they should engage students in the development of the essential skills and traits that they will need to succeed as 21st century learners.

Using mediums to advantage

The pedagogogical structure of a WebQuest lends itself to several different media, not just static web pages and links to newspaper articles. Links can be to videos, podcasts, infographics, social media, or even some offline content. However, a WebQuest that can be done completely offline does not exploit the digital or technological media that is available to teachers and students today, and is simply no more than a worksheet-based activity that might contain some internet links.

Scaffolding great expectations

Scaffolding learning through the selection of various resources and task requirements allows learners to build upon previous schema and to work together to develop content that they may not otherwise have been able to produce.

There are three kinds of scaffolding commonly employed in a WebQuest: reception, transformation, and production (Dodge, 2001). The reception aspect puts students in contact with resources that they may not have chosen or used before, and requires a level of guidance to be incorporated into the process of making meaning or learning from the content. Types of this content might include guides, tips, glossaries, or a thesaurus. The transformation aspect requires students to change what they read, see, hear, or experience into a new form of knowledge.; for example recognizing a pattern in data, finding comparisons or contrasts across several media elements, engaging in brainstorming, participating in decision making, or conducting inductive reasoning. Essentially, the production aspect will see students develop or create something that did not previously exist. To complete such tasks, the use of templates, prompted writing guides, and various multimedia elements is imperative. Example end products include something as complex as a cookbook that consists of various culturally-based recipes, a magazine consisting of various articles, and the development of a three minute book trailer or a yearly highlights reel.

How do I craft a WebQuest?

To begin to develop a WebQuest, it's a good idea to focus on each section one at a time.

Introduction/Description
Introduce the WebQuest to students by writing the WebQuest with the students as the audience. Provide an overview, and set up any role-playing scenarios in this section. In other words, this section should be used to prepare the students for the tasks that they need to undertake, and provide an overview of the lesson and activities. To capture student interest regarding the topic, use a motivational 'hook' or a captivating question.

Task
This is where you will state the end results of students' activities by informing them of what tasks they must achieve by the end of the Webquest.

Tasks might be comprised of elements such as
- a series of questions,
- a number of problems that require solving, or
- sides of an argument that must be formulated and then defended.

Keep in mind that tasks need to focus on students' being able to work with the material to gain an understanding of the arguments and positions, and then formulate their own opinion and understanding of the topic.

Process

In this section, list a step-by-step process for students to follow when completing the assigned task(s) by elaborating on how it/they can be achieved. Guidance on how to organize and present the information should also be included here. A checklist can be provided that highlights important points and concepts that students need to understand in order to complete each task. Also include any suggestions and advice on how to structure and organize the material for what will be the ultimate result of the project, and how you would like students to present the material, such as summary tables and graphs.

Resources

All of the resources required for completing the WebQuest need to be provided to students from the outset, and can either be incorporated in the 'Process' section or included in their own section. Resources include all webpage links, and any additional media (including audio, video, and textbooks) that students will be expected to access in order to complete their assigned task(s). Ideally, each resource item when listed should also contain a brief annotation so that students know what the link or resource is referring to and how it can assist them in completing the task.

Evaluation

A rubric to assess students in their completion of the task, and their understanding of the content worked through, needs to be developed. Students should be presented with the rubric so they have an understanding of what is expected of them, and how they will be assessed.

Conclusion

In the final section of the WebQuest, students need to present or submit the results of their task(s) for assessment. In this section also, the teacher needs to provide students with reflection on the topic either by using rhetorical questions or by asking discussion-based questions that help transfer the knowledge gained through completion of the WebQuest to a broader context, as well as into other aspects of the local teaching and learning environment.

How would I use a tool to create a WebQuest?

Once designed and set up, a WebQuest is essentially a worksheet or a web page laid out in a particular format. However, it is much more than just a 'lesson planning form' to be filled in; it is a self-contained learning unit that students can follow, explore, and complete. A WebQuest can therefore be developed as a web page in a learning management system (LMS) like Edmodo, Moodle, or Schoology. Alternatively, a WebQuest could be posted to a social networking site under a group that students could join. The WebQuest could also be run from a hard drive with all files saved locally. In any of these cases, all that is required is that the media, and any follow-up links intended for use in the process section, are posted and are readily accessible by students.

Websites that allow the hosting and authoring of WebQuests by teachers are also available. QuestGarden and Zunal are two, and both offer the online authoring of a WebQuest, and the hosting of it so that other teachers can search and use the learning material as well. However, while WebQuests are available on a number of topics from these websites, any content developed by other teachers should be assessed for suitability with your own classes, teaching style, and students, and modified accordingly.

While QuestGarden follows the WebQuest model very strictly, Zunal allows for the inclusion of a number of additional resources whiche include adding games, pre- and post-tests, and Google Map-based activities. Both sites are free to start and have a membership or pro account option available as an upgrade. QuestGarden and Zunal are similar to each other and have their own advantages as a WebQuest hosting or creation service. QuestGarden has been around the longest, while Zunal is a more recent addition to the WebQuest community.

The choice is yours, but please keep in mind that tools and websites do at times change the features that they offer and the layout of the interface. Some may even become defunct.

The following guides have been written in a way that any such changes will not impact on understanding the essential mechanisms behind the use of the WebQuest model, nor on the development of a good WebQuest using any available web-based template.

QuestGarden

Preparation

QuestGarden allows for a 30-day free trial before there is a need to subscribe to a 2-year membership. Any WebQuests created during the trial period will remain active and available after the trial ends, so that they can be downloaded in a zip file for hosting elsewhere if desired. The QuestGarden site allows you to search for, and use, existing WebQuests created by other teachers, and it allows you to use them as-is or to modify them.

You can create one of your own as well. The tutorial here will cover the process of creating a WebQuest of your own.

Step One – Getting started

To get started with the QuestGarden website, sign up for a free trial by going to the homepage and clicking on 'Register for a free trial'. The free trial allows for the creation of an unlimited amount of WebQuests, and for them to be downloaded in a zip file if needed (even after the trial period is over). The paid membership feature allows for WebQuest editing and creation past the trial period, and access to a wider range of templates for WebQuest creation. However, once you have signed up, a site profile will need to be created. Your personal information can then be entered, after which you will be taken to the 'Member dashboard'.

Step Two – Exploring the site

After becoming a member, there are several site options to explore. You can 'Learn about WebQuests' by going over the videos hosted on the site by Bernie Dodge – videos discussing good examples, and the common development mistakes made when creating a WebQuest. You can choose to click on 'Collaborate with others' to see who is currently online, and make comments on WebQuest as they are being developed. Otherwise, you may simply want to take some time to search for examples on a specific topic.

Step Three – Search for examples

Prior to the development of a WebQuest, it is a good idea to review others until you are comfortable with the format and the expectations associated with their development. Click 'Search for examples' to begin looking for WebQuests by keyword, or by specific grade and curriculum area. It is also possible to conduct a search based on a WebQuest design pattern (for example, alternate history, persuasive message, travel plan). After you feel comfortable with the type of WebQuests on offer from the site, and have gained enough familiarity with the site after navigating through all of its resources, you may want to start to develop your own WebQuest for the site to host.

Step Four – Creation: Template use

Click 'Create a WebQuest' then 'Click here' to begin editing your first WebQuest for hosting on QuestGarden. A template will then be provided that will walk you through the major sections of creation. These include looking at the 'Goals and context' of the WebQuest (for example, the topic, curriculum standards, and the teaching and learning environment), any associated 'Task and assessment' elements (for example, the problem that students will address), the 'Process' that students will engage in (for example, the how and when of the resources they will use), and any other 'Final details' (for example, an introduction and conclusion, and how the work can be adapted for use by other teachers). Further options include adding 'Polish' to the WebQuest (for example, adjusting the layout and adding images to enhance the presentation for learners), as well as some necessary distribution and hosting 'Tools' (for example, 'Preview', Publish', 'Export', and 'Read comments').

Step Five – Goals and context

In this section of the template, you will need to initially choose a design pattern from the list provided and click 'Select'. After that, you will be presented with an example format that illustrates how each section will guide you. After reviewing this information, click on 'Title/authors/group' to enter these details, information such as a description of your WebQuest, and a record of the grade level and the curriculum area associated with it. Click on 'Standards' to add the standards covered by the WebQuest, and 'Learners' to enter further information about the students intended to undertake the WebQuest. You will then come across 'Checkpoint 1', which can be used to make notes regarding aspects of any part of the materials that need to be improved, and for making general comments about this stage of the lesson. Any comments that are made here will appear in the comments section of the lesson.

Step Six – Task and assessment

In this section of the template, click on 'Introduction' to get started on writing the introduction for the WebQuest, and 'Task' to input elements of the learners' end goal(s), and the focus of their activities. 'Evaluation' will then allow you to edit an existing four-point rubric to suit your own teaching and learning context. This will see you reach 'Checkpoint 2', which allows you to confirm that the task and the evaluations marry up, and that the task is an appropriate one for the WebQuest. As in Checkpoint 1, any comments created under here will also appear in the lesson comments section.

Step Seven – Process

The 'Process' section starts out with a reminder of the importance of finding suitable web-based resources for the learner audience. There is space for three different processes, 'Process 1', 'Process 2', and 'Process 3', and each of these areas allows you to enter the steps involved with each process and the required resources. As with the previous section, all details are entered into the WYSIWYG (what you see is what you get) html editor, with the example tabs providing some support for use of the pattern selected. Again, you are able to see a design view, source view, or a preview of the information being edited, and you must click 'Save' in order to store the information before moving on to the next area or section. Once completed, 'Checkpoint 3' will be reached, and again, comments left here will be visible on the lesson comments section of the WebQuest.

A number of questions are posed so that checks can be made concerning the learning material developed for this section and the appropriateness of its use with students.

Step Eight – Final Details

The 'Final details' section allows for the development of a 'Conclusion', along with a 'Teacher Intro', 'Teacher resources', 'Teacher process', and 'Credits' areas. The 'Conclusion' needs to focus on elements such as a summary of the goals and details of the WebQuest, and take into account student reflection on their learning. You could also provide links to areas of further study for students as well. The remaining areas are for you to complete with information that can be used by other teachers, so that they can see how your WebQuest can be adaptable or useable in their teaching and learning contexts. Now you come to 'Checkpoint 4' which gives you a chance to review all elements of this section with guided questions, and where, as before, any comments will be visible in the lesson comment area.

Step Nine – Polish and finalization

In the 'Polish' section there is an area available to 'Add images' where there are several links to a number of image resource sites, and a small example of how to use the WYSIWIG editor to add an image to the WebQuest. Clicking 'Appearance' will open up a new browser window or tab so that you can see your WebQuest and make adjustments to the appearance of the titles, headers, navigation bar, body text, and links. 'Checkpoint 5' is the last of the checkpoints, and like all the others before it, provides some guided questions to help you think about how you have developed this section of the WebQuest, and how you can improve upon it if necessary. Your WebQuest is now complete, but there are several site tools that are important to review.

Step Ten – Tools

The 'Tools' section of the template offers 'Preview', 'Publish', 'Export' and 'Read comments' areas. Click on 'Preview' to open a new browser window or tab to see how others will view the completed WebQuest when it is hosted. The 'Publish' section allows you to publish your Webquest, and there are several choices which include keeping either the URL of the WebQuest known to only yourself or making it available to others, and granting permission for your material to be used by other teachers. A tiny URL can also be created here by paid subscribers. The 'Export' option allows you to download a zip file of your WebQuest, and any comments that have been made on the WebQuest can be viewed here (including your own). You can also reply to any comments from this page.

Zunal

Preparation

Zunal is free to register, and offers its service to pre- and in-service teachers as well as faculty to create and share WebQuests with each other. The Zunal site allows you to search for and use existing WebQuests created by other teachers, and it allows you to use them as-is, or to create your own using their online template. By registering with the site, you have a free account which allows you to create just one WebQuest. To create more you need to select an upgrade to a pro-account, which allows you to not only create additional WebQuests, but it allows you to copy and enhance other WebQuests, present ad free WebQuests, and add additional modules to your WebQuests (for example, a quiz, a Google Map-based activity, games like hangman, or additional blank pages). A group account is also possible as a special subscription option. Nonetheless, the tutorial here will cover the process behind the creation of a single WebQuest using the free account type.

Step One – Getting Started

To get started with the Zunal website go to the home page and click 'Register'. After entering your details and registering, you will be taken to the 'My profile' page.

Step Two – Exploring the site

After becoming a member, there are several site options to explore. You can begin by expanding your profile, or changing the information thatyou have entered about yourself (for example, your school, your photo, or your password). You can also upgrade or delete your account from here. This page also allows you to view, delete, or update the WebQuests you have created, see a list of any WebQuests that you have made favorites, and develop your own WebQuest. The menu options along the top of the screen allow you to 'Browse' the WebQuests available by curriculum and grade level, browse a 'Help' question and answer page, or ask 'Questions' about, or provide suggestions for, the Zunal WebQuest Maker. An option to return to the 'My dashboard' is available from the top menu as well.

Step Three – Search the site

Prior to the development of a WebQuest it is a good idea to review others until you are comfortable with the format and the expectations associated with their development. From the top level menu, click on 'Browse', and from this page you will be able to see how many WebQuests are available by grade level and curriculum. You can click to explore the WebQuests available for each, or alternatively you can click on the 'Search' tab to perform a keyword search with or without curriculum and grade level as operators. After you have completed a few searches, reviewed several of the WebQuests available, and feel comfortable with the type of WebQuests on offer, you may want to develop your own WebQuest for the site to host.

Step Four – Creation: Template use

To start creating a WebQuest at Zunal, click on 'Create a WebQuest' from the 'My Dashboard' page, then 'Create a WebQuest from scratch', and enter a title for your WebQuest. (Alternatively, if you are a pro-member, you can copy and enhance a WebQuest).

Step Five – The WebQuest template page

After entering a title for your WebQuest, you will be taken to the WebQuest template page. Along the top, you will be able to see the title of your WebQuest as well as 'Add to favorites' and 'Preview mode'. Along the left side, you will find three areas of buttons, one for developing the WebQuest (from the introduction to the conclusion), one consisting of various tools relating to the WebQuest (for example, statistics and exporting features), and an area for pro-members called 'Add to your WebQuest' (which includes a settings and publishing feature, as well as various additional modules that you can use to add value to your WebQuest like including games, quizzes, and Google Map-based activities). In the center of the screen is a WYSIWIG (What You See Is What You Get) HTML editor where the results of your editing and your WebQuest appear. Directly below that is an 'Add resource button' that will allow you to upload various documents and links, and directly below that again is the public URL of the WebQuest you are going to create.

Step Six – Developing the WebQuest

On entering the WebQuest template page, you will be at the 'Welcome' screen of your WebQuest. It is here where you can update the 'WebQuest Information', which includes adding a description, and some keywords, and identifying the appropriate grade level and curriculum area for its use. If you wish to add a welcoming image, click on 'Update image' to upload one from your computer; click on 'Update WebQuest

Information' to change the name, description, grade level, curriculum, keywords, and author; click on 'Add resources' to add a content section, website URLs, local files, local photos, videos from other websites (including YouTube, and TeacherTube), a Voki, or a Glogster poster; and then click on 'Preview Mode' to see how the WebQuest will appear. 'Admin mode' will return you to editing. When you are happy with the welcome screen, you can begin to work on the other elements of the WebQuest.

Step Seven – Introduction

To begin working on the other elements of the WebQuest, click on the appropriate button in the developing WebQuest area (for example, introduction, task, process, evaluation, conclusion, or teacher page). After clicking on 'introduction', you will be able to follow a similar process as that of creating the 'Welcome' page. Information, in the form of 'Help', is provided to guide in the development of the elements for the Introduction. After reading the help provided, click 'Update content', and you will be presented with four sections to complete.

- 'Advice to teachers' – to describe the WebQuest, the amount of time it should take to deliver, and other details for teachers who may want to use or adapt the content with their classes.
- 'Standards' – where you can enter the list of standards that the WebQuest addresses.
- 'Credits' – where you can thank others and provide permission for content or resource usage.
- 'Other' – to add further information if needed.

Once you have completed these sections, click 'Save now' and you will be returned to the 'Introduction' page of the template. You will then be able to 'Update image' or 'Add resources' to the section if you wish, and you can also 'Reset' the page', 'Rename' the page, 'Hide' the page, and move the page 'Up' and 'Down' within the order of presentation.

Step Eight – Task

After completing the 'Introduction' section of the template, click on 'Task' to continue building the WebQuest. Here, you will be provided with some help, in the form of text to guide you in the development of this section (just as in the introduction). When you are ready to enter the appropriate details for the section, click on 'Update content' and you will be taken to a basic WYSIWIG editor. At the bottom of the editor are the definitions of a task, an example, and a rubric to help you in task development. Once you have entered the task elements, previewed them if necessary, and are happy with them, click 'Save now' to record the changes and return to the WebQuest template page. You can then 'Update image' or 'Update resources' for the task if you wish, and continue to the 'Process' section of the WebQuest template.

Step Nine – Process

Click on 'Process' and you will be taken to the process page where you will be guided in text form, as in the previous pages. When ready you can click on 'Update content' to begin adding elements and reviewing them in a similar manner as previous sections. When you have checked the page in 'Preview mode' and you are satisfied, return to 'Admin mode' and 'Update image' or 'Add resources' before moving on to the 'Evaluation' section.

Step Ten – Evaluation

Click on 'Evaluation' to begin editing this section using the template. Once again, you will be provided with help in the form of text, and the means to edit the section in the same manner as previous sections. There is also the ability to edit a provided rubric template, but you will need to change the 'Ratings', the 'Category of assessment' and the factors that align the categories to the ratings, and a possible 'score'. Obviously, you may upload a link, a file, or an image of your own rubric if you choos and you would need to click 'Hide rubric' so that the provided template rubric is not shown. After you have previewed the page, you can move on to the next section of the template.

Step Eleven – Conclusion and teacher page

Click on 'Conclusion' to begin editing the final section of the WebQuest for students. As in previous sections, you will be provided with help in the form of text, and the means to edit the section in the way described previously. After returning to the WebQuest template, the 'Teacher page' is the next option to click after conclusion where the details for this section can be (and should have been already) entered from the 'Welcome' page. If not, or if changes need to be applied, then you can do these now by clicking on the 'Teacher page', and then editing the section in a similar fashion as all of those previous. Congratulations! The WebQuest, and notes for any other teacher who may wish to use it, is now complete and ready for use with students.

Step Twelve – Tools of the WebQuest

Of course, having a ready WebQuest would not be complete without being able to at least share or review it, and this is where the tools of the WebQuest section are important. This section consists of 'About the author(s)', 'Evaluate the WebQuest', 'Reviews', 'Statistics', 'Export the Webquest', and 'Share this WebQuest'. Click 'About the author(s)' and then 'Update profile information' or add another author if you want to share development of the WebQuest. Click on 'Evaluate WebQuest' to provide a self-evaluation of the WebQuest using a pre-fabricated rubric. The rubric is lengthy and very detailed, so it might be wise to click 'Print rubric' to go over a hard copy if required. Click on 'Reviews' to see the number of reviews, approved reviews, and reviews awaiting approval. You can also click on 'Write a review' to provide a star rating (from 1 to 5) to accompany it. Click 'Statistics' to see details of the level of completion for each section of the WebQuest in terms of percent. Click 'Export WebQuest' to export the WebQuest in one of three formats: Adobe PDF, Microsoft Word, or Microsoft Excel. Finally, click 'Share this WebQuest' to distribute the WebQuest via email, over Facebook, on Twitter, or on Digg.

What are the key points behind WebQuest use in the TESOL context?

Working with WebQuests, particularly those developed for use with second-language learners of English, sees several important key points emerge:

- WebQuests need to be used as inquiry-oriented learning tools.
- WebQuests are extremely teacher-directed and planned; yet they are intensely student-centered.
- WebQuests, depending on their length, have very different learning goals, and exist as short and long-term types.
- WebQuests need to be developed in ways that seek to engage, motiveate, and go beyond rote thinking for learners.
- WebQuests expose learners to authentic material, develop their collaboration skills, and enhance their communicative opportunities and abilities.
- WebQuests follow a well-established format.

- WebQuests are most suited to tasks involving creativity and problems with several possible solutions.
- WebQuest websites can be relied upon as go to authoring tools and depositiories for the creation and housing of WebQuest content.
- WebQuest content can be saved offline, and can be provided to students as an offline activity in environments where continued access to the internet is problematic.

At the end of the day, WebQuests, although developed in the very early days of the internet, have proven themselves to still be relevant to teaching and learning, and they remain adaptable to student needs as well as the curriculum. WebQuests also allow for the teacher to create material that focuses on student development in engaging and motivating ways that can, in turn, inspire collaboration, creativity, and language development.

3. Constructing Visually-based Asynchronous Conversations: VoiceThreading

3. Constructing Visually-based Asynchronous Conversations: VoiceThreading

Overview

VoiceThread firmly establishes itself as a tool that has the exciting potential to give an actual audible voice to those language students who rarely, if ever, speak the target language in class, and it does so by providing students with the means to construct visually-based digital conversations. In light of this, the pedagogical affordances provided by this web-based tool are considered within this book, along with the types of educational VoiceThreads that are in use today. The efficacy behind VoiceThread development, with and for students, is then oriented toward the teaching of English to speakers of other languages (TESOL) with a brief overview of VoiceThread instructional strategies that are suited to second-language learners of English, supported by example activities and resources. A means of evaluating language production and learning outcomes afforded through use of the tool then follows, along with an overview of the techniques essential for monitoring, producing, and guiding effective VoiceThread development among language learners. A tutorial for getting started with the technology, and developing visually-based digital conversations, is also provided, along with a variety of other useful resources to assist students and teachers as they begin to participate in VoiceThreading.

What is a VoiceThread?

VoiceThread is an asynchronous online tool and associated mobile application that employs uploaded audio comments, a narrating tool, text balloons, and web-cam video annotation to support the online discussion of media artifacts. These media artifacts can consist of documents, images, presentations or videos. The tool allows for moderated feedback, which in turn allows both instructors and students to control the dissemination of feedback in terms of monitoring postings for inappropriate content. Most importantly, after creation, VoiceThreads are immediately web-accessible and can be embedded into other websites including blogs, wikis, and course management systems like Moodle, thereby supporting student accessibility across a range of platforms (Pacansky-Brock, 2013). To date, VoiceThread has proved useful in a number of educational contexts from second language learning (Bush, 2009; Akasha, 2011; Pallos & Pallos, 2011; Sun, Yu, & Gao, 2013) to literacy development (Smith & Dobson, 2009) as well as in use with adults and young learners alike (Gillis, Luthin, Parette, & Blum, 2012; Lewis, Burks, Shumack & Shumack, 2014).

VoiceThread was originally launched in 2007, and today, it allows for navigation between slides and comment postings in five different ways: using voice with a microphone, using voice by telephone, typing text, uploading an audio file, or by making a webcam video. Postings can be augmented with the use of a narration drawing tool during the recording process. Any created VoiceThread can then be shared with friends, groups of learners or colleagues, and they in turn can leave comments on the thread or edit it (if the necessary permissions allow).

How can I use VoiceThread?

VoiceThread was not specifically designed to be used as an educational tool, and while the functionality of a number of the applications features do not always marry with pedagogy, it is possible to match many VoiceThread features with pedagogical affordances (Burden & Atkinson, 2008), including:

- focusing learner attention on specifics via the zoom tool;
- providing formative feedback on media related content emerging from asynchronous comments pertaining to thread artifact(s);
- learner communities can visualize and provide responses to cumulative postings, as users can post comments reflecting on other users comments;
- instant feedback can be provided from a potentially global audience, as the thread can be made viewable by anyone online;
- comment moderation, which allows the thread to be managed and monitored for appropriateness; and
- an 'at once' visual overview of content (rather rather than a long text-based thread) which stems from capturing a full discussion on a single page.

The VoiceThread context also affords students with an environment from which to work collaboratively to communicate and engage in learning, while teachers can utilize the tool for creation, discussion, assessment, or even in a flipped classroom context (Hughes, 2012; Nicholson, 2013; Moore, Gillet & Steele, 2014).

VoiceThreads provide a creative outlet for students that encourages idea sharing, and this can potentially allow students to learn more about others' experiences and views as they explore the thinking of others through images, text, use of narration drawing tools, and voice. Instead of the traditional, which may be full of teacher-talk or conversations on a turn-by-turn basis, VoiceThreads can maintain multiple discussion strands, and as responses can be made asynchronously, learners have more time to absorb each strand and develop more complex thought out responses to each of them. VoiceThreads make it easy to see what students contribute and how much effort they put into producing the comments that they create. In turn, these comments allow teachers to see if students understand the key concepts that are being studied, as learners begin to put things into their own words and make comments on peers and teacher VoiceThread content and contributions. As a result, many different types of VoiceThread have emerged.

The extensive use of VoiceThread by educators today has prompted the emergence of a significant research base around the use of the tool, as well as sites like the Voicethread 4 Education wiki to emerge. This wiki has come to provide a library of VoiceThread examples from which to gather potential pedagogical uses and ideas, along with examples of best practice.

What type of educational VoiceThreads exist?

As VoiceThreads can be used to share information, start discussions, receive feedback, or simply tell a story, Poelzer (2009) along with Elwood (2010) recognize the educational opportunities that VoiceThread can provide, and the strategies required for its effective use as a learning tool – particularly for the creation of digital storytelling projects, demonstrating knowledge gained in research or inquiry projects, documenting student progress over time, and sharing information with an authentic audience. Poelzer also views VoiceThread as extremely adaptable, and as useful for a multitude of purposes across a range of subjects and curriculums, as numerous subject areas can be integrated within a single VoiceThread which, as Dyck (2007) points out, can be used to develop storytelling and deep thinking skills, as well as communication skills, or even used as a means to conduct assessment. A number of different types of VoiceThread use by educators has emerged (Pires, 2010), including:

- collaborative digital storytelling creation,
- discussion, suggestion, and opinion activities,
- problem solving skill development tasks,
- peer review,
- keyword identification,
- image notation and captioning,
- revision work completion,
- book and movie review development,
- digital portfolio construction,
- as well as comic strip building.

Burden and Atkinson (2008) also identify a number of activities suitable for VoiceThread use, from stimulus, narrative, collaborative, conceptual, empathic, and representational. Such as:

- video posting without sound, with learners commenting on what might be being said;
- presenting the first half of a video clip, and then asking learners to predict what might happen next; or
- assigning different roles to students, and having them post comments assuming the perspectives of that role.

Going one step further, Vesper (2008) provides a series of examples of effective practice that includes using VoiceThread as a tool to extend the literacy and numeracy skills of students; allow for the showcasing and evaluation of student work;

develop collaborative skills amongst students; and provide for the career building options of teachers. Student literacy skills can be developed by presenting written texts in oral form, creating poetry anthologies and book reviews, constructing choose-your-own-adventure stories (which can be augmented with student generated artwork, with narration and text, to extend the creativity and collaboration aspects), writing stories to go with images, exploring 'what if' variations of video clips, and creating instructions or showing the steps in a process to match media artifacts. Numeracy skills can be enhanced through development of math games and problem solving puzzles, focusing on real life problem solving situations, and representing mathematical concepts visually. Showcasing and evaluating work can be achieved by preparing digital portfolios and goal setting, while taking part in collaborative projects involves students' thinking around topics, and providing commentary and debate on the issues, and then summarizing class discussions and research within a VoiceThread. Career building for teachers can also occur with VoiceThread by allowing teachers to house and provide classroom teaching content for students, engage in the delivery of professional development, and share ideas between colleagues and then critically reflect on aspects of the ideas presented.

What elements are behind an effective VoiceThread?

If you are new to VoiceThreading, then to see what constitutes the creation of an effective VoiceThread, you can begin by experimenting. You could start out by commenting on a few existing VoiceThreads before creating a couple of practice threads yourself. After viewing several, and leaving a comment or two here and there, start by creating a VoiceThread that is small, contains only a few artifacts, and focuses on a single activity or topic.

Creating an initial VoiceThread should begin with an understanding of the direction in which you wish to take it. After that, media artifacts should be selected that will promote or lead the VoiceThread in this direction. Also, when creating a VoiceThread as an example for students, provide model comments. This is particularly important as many students need examples so that they know what is expected of them when making their comments and replies. Just be sure to select and prepare content so that it is engaging and will lead to potential interaction. See the resource notes on incorporating and constructing a VoiceThread in Chapter 14 for an overview to follow in initial VoiceThread construction for classroom use.

If you intend to have students create their own VoiceThreads, then be sure to provide topics that allow room for student creativity to emerge, as this can lead to more thoughtful and interesting comments. Keep pedagogy in mind, and ensure that a solid learning outcome can develop from student participation and involvement with the VoiceThread process. It may prove best to start students off in pairs or groups, as this can help promote brainstorming and prove effective for them to draft any initial comments for the associated topic they have chosen or been provided. This also helps ensure that the very first comments that students produce follow the intention of the VoiceThread, and are on topic and well thought out, particularly since they are composed with teacher assistance. It also ensures that all students have, at the very least, one comment to place on their VoiceThread and, as such, can become familiar with the basic means of the commenting process. This also encourages students with low in-class participation to begin to contribute equally to the project. However, perhaps limit initial participation to a small group for each thread, as this can later be expanded as students become used to the site and get better at moderating comments and filtering content. If so desired, the VoiceThread can then be opened up to other users and stakeholders such as parents, and if the teaching context allows for it, it can be open to anyone at all, as this can provide potential incoming comments containing naturally spoken language from a global audience.

After students have created their own VoiceThreads, it is important that you become involved in each one. Ensure that you are invited to every student-created VoiceThread so that you can provide any necessary guidance, advice, structure, or authority and most importantly, monitor development and provide filtering. Don't just leave the provision of comments up to the students; keep modeling appropriate content for students to mirror by focusing on style, structure, language use, grammar, length, and anything else that you may consider to be an important aspect to tailor for that particular class or group of students. To further assist in generating appropriate and effective student comments, it may prove necessary to enforce guidelines which will guarantee that student participation is controlled and secured by structuring expected content. Continuously aim to provide teacher direction, but also maintain a student-centered learning environment through the promotion of student autonomy. Assist learners in identifying content and comments that are inappropriate, and be sure to monitor all comments so that any inappropriate content can be filtered out immediately. Establish an expected standard of quality, and assist students in being able to reach that level. Hold students accountable for their online work, and help them to truly understand that the work they create is going out to a wider audience than just the classroom teacher and their classmates, and that it is work that can be accessed at any time (not just during class or school hours).

It is also advisable to spotlight student comments. This allows teachers to reinforce comments that are effective and stimulate the growth of a VoiceThread, and to see that students produce comments that stick to the main topic of the thread. Spotlighting can also empower learners and spur motivation while highlighting material that students are expected to produce. Poor comments can prove to be effective examples to highlight, where comments that might be considered 'throw away', or ones that students make to just fulfill the commenting task are targeted. This can drive home the notion that such comments that are meaningless are both unconstructive and are not useful or highly valued in digital spaces (Hoskins Sakamoto, 2010). That said, when highlighting poor comments, it is also important to indicate how these comments can best be improved.

Several other factors to consider include: access, paid account use, stable hardware and internet connections, reliance on reusable content, and practicing the safe-guarding of students.

The means by which your classroom provides access to computers and the internet will largely dictate the possibilities of VoiceThread use. Some teachers may have a single computer in the room which is tied to an interactive whiteboard or beam projector. Other teachers may have to schedule computer lab time at their school before they can gain access to computers for student use, while other students may only be able to access computers at home and not at all in the teaching context.

If using a paid account, a number of teacher aliases can be created under the one account and this can assist in monitoring students and grouping them with ease. However, paid accounts can prove to be expensive, even those that are 'educator priced', and you should be sure that VoiceThread is a technology that you consider actually worth your own personal investment if paying out-of-pocket.

Also keep in mind that VoiceThreads are an online dependent technology, and must be accessed with a reliable internet connection from a computer or table device that is capable of accessing the internet efficiently. In relation to this, you must prepare a contingency plan to cover any internet outage or technological breakdowns if you are to use VoiceThread in the classroom during work hours. This notion also ties into the need to ensure that the hardware to be used must be in good working order and accessible at the appropriate times – for example, by confirming computer lab bookings or in a bring-your-own-device (BYOD) setting confirm that the devices are actually brought to school. Students must also have access to any planned data that they will use to create their VoiceThreads, and carrying this on a USB stick or being able to access it from a shared folder on a network or other computer is necessary.

Further, you shouldn't be reinventing the wheel each time that you start a VoiceThread project. Previously created VoiceThreads can be used over and over again, and examples of student created work can be saved or exported as examples of best practice. With this in mind, copyright issues are also important. Students may need to be reminded or taught about aspects of educational fair use as well as plagiarism. This is especially true of young learners, but even of some adults. It may prove necessary to provide a citation or reference list in a word file on the last slide of each VoiceThread that students create, even if only for the sake of practice.

Finally, always safeguard students, and constantly monitor all student-created VoiceThreads for inappropriate content and/or comments. Further, ensure that young learners do not upload photographs of themselves or use their full names, or any private personal data when making comments. In this regard, students in the English as a foreign language (EFL) context may prove better off using their English nicknames when working with VoiceThread projects. So too, in some teaching contexts, it will be necessary to gain parent permission before students can participate in any use of a VoiceThread.

How can VoiceThread lend itself to TESOL?

A number of possibilities exist for utilizing VoiceThread in the teaching of English to speakers of other languages. Students can participate in speaking and listening activities when recording or responding to a VoiceThread; teachers can set topic-based presentations or dialog-based conversational tasks; and classes can share projects with other classes, allowing them to see what other students are studying and to provide comments on that group of learners who then respond in turn. It also allows students to provide a window into their experiences and ideas, and it allows stakeholders (administrators, teachers, parents, and the students themselves) to monitor the learning outcomes and the educational product that emerges.

As the VoiceThread website (VoiceThread, 2016) itself states that 'participation is not optional', it appears that VoiceThread has established itself as a tool that any EFL educator can immediately recognize as having the exciting potential that gives an actual audible voice to those students who rarely, or if ever, speak in class. It also provides a voice for those unwilling to speak out in front of peers, and if such students still feel too uncomfortable to actually verbalize their thoughts or responses in a second language, then they can always retain the option to type comments. As such, if the focus of the lesson is on speaking and pronunciation, as it is many times in the language classroom, then you may inform students that they can use any option but the keyboard to comment. Leaving spoken comments on a VoiceThread can break down the affective filters that many learners carry with them into language classrooms (Hacker, 2010). On the other hand, if the focus is on reading and writing, then students can limit their comments to writing and notation if deemed necessary.

In this respect, for English language learners, VoiceThread comes to afford a number of opportunities to engage in online discussion while practicing speaking and writing skills asynchronously. This comes to support a multiple intelligence approach to learning and helps encourage participation and build learner confidence by providing time for students to reflect and construct responses before posting (Recchio-Demmin, 2009).

How can I start using VoiceThread with students?

An important resource that is introduced in Chapter 3, and one where TESOL educators can gain insight into the myriad uses of VoiceThread in education, is that provided by Cassinelli (2016). The VoiceThread 4 education wiki provides an extremely comprehensive collection of examples from educators and instructors of all ages and academic backgrounds, including those from the K-12 environment, the tertiary education sector, special education, and the English as a foreign language (EFL) and English as a second language (ESL) context. A few examples, with extension ideas, from that web site include creating discussions based on themes or genres (such as emotions or music), allowing students to introduce their hometowns, countries, or even themselves and their family in a VoiceThread, as well as creating an international collaborative project based on food image postings – with students from one country inviting students from other countries to comment on food images and provide recipes and their own food postings as well. VoiceThreads can also be useful in teaching the alphabet to young learners. Hoskins Sakamoto (2010) has applied VoiceThread to make an alphabet book which has a photo for each letter, and students make the letter shapes with their bodies. The pages also contain audio comments from students as they pronounce each letter and match it to an English word, for example, 'a, a, apple; b, b, bird'. The 'book' can be exported and provided to students at the end of the alphabet, so they each have a personal copy of the project. Such a project can prove valuable for extending lesson outcomes as it allows for other teachers and students around the world to comment on each of the 'letter' pages. Students can therefore gain increased exposure to a range of different native and non-native English speaking accents as well as providing teaching opportunities associated with speaker country of origin, and perhaps also vocabulary. Such a project would be a common one in EFL and ESL classrooms alike, and through the use of VoiceThread, opportunities exist for comments to be made from children in native-English speaking countries. Such children can also produce their own alphabet book in response, or provide more vocabulary for each letter. So too, parents can be provided with the link so that the material can be practiced at home for reinforcement.

In fact, almost any classroom content can be ported to a VoiceThread context for use as a potential language learning activity. VoiceThread is particularly well-suited as a means from which students can introduce themselves using images, videos, and text excerpts of favorite books or poems, as well as providing details of their hobbies, background information on their friends, family, pets, and even their favorite places to relax or to go on vacation. Other traditional activity uses of VoiceThread can include focusing students on a single topic by having them present on popular social issues or issues of interest to them, providing a book or film review, or using it to tell a progressive 'Chinese whisper' type story. In such a story, the teacher begins by adding an initial image to a VoiceThread and making the first comment, with the students in turn adding their images and comments to extend the story, and the teacher adding a final image and a closing comment. Other VoiceThreads containing images may be set up to allow students to extract information from the photographs presented by asking *wh*-questions (Who? What? When? Where? Why? How?). To expand the deeper thinking skills of students, they can then be directed to focus on examining the images in more detail, and commenting on what influences may have impacted upon elements in the image when it was taken, and how these relate to the world today. Such a process can also assist in helping students gain the language skills required to tell complex stories through the use of picture and narration. Taking the theme of thinking skills one step further, clue-based games may be developed with one group of students preparing an image montage that can be uploaded to a VoiceThread to provide hints for a question or riddle that students ask as a comment. Other students can then make their own comment on the VoiceThread to guess the answer to the riddle, before uploading their own hint montage and riddle. Answers can then be provided in class, or by making an answer comment at a set date or on the final slide of the VoiceThread so that the solution can be discovered at any time.

Other potentially exciting uses of VoiceThread involve employing it to teach directions, housing dialog-based language learning activities, or using the mandated textbook more creatively. In teaching directions, images can be zoomed in on and panned around freely, and this allows for various directions to be stated and followed with ease. An image of a map can be uploaded to the VoiceThread with a teacher comment asking for directions (for example, How do I get to the supermarket?). This initial comment should be followed by an example model comment, illustrating how to get to the supermarket and any special vocabulary (Go straight for two blocks then take a right, continue straight, and you'll see the supermarket on the left). Further, when housing dialog-based language learning activities, a VoiceThread can be set up with an initial image to provide an overview of the topic or language situation presented. Students can then engage in a conversational turn-taking dialog. For example, a picture of a restaurant can be uploaded with two students engaging in a conversation as waiter and customer, with images and comments uploaded to suit the progression of the topic as the conversation evolves. Alternatively, as the conversation evolves, other students can take over the turn-taking process. In this case, a second pair of students acting as the same waiter and customer could then add a menu image with the customer asking for advice on what to order or asking for more details about a certain dish. A third pair may continue the waiter-customer dialog by experiencing a problem (such as a fly in the soup) or simply asking for and paying the bill. Where a pre-selected textbook must be used and followed meticulously over a preplanned course of study (as is the case in many middle and high schools), parts of the textbook can be scanned by teachers and inserted into a VoiceThread so that students can provide spoken answers to the questions that are asked in the text. This technique can also be augmented so that students can complete any associated textbook homework on lesson content via a single VoiceThread, with this VoiceThread then coming to serve as an assessment e-portfolio tool.

How do I evaluate a VoiceThread?

For VoiceThreads, the rubric presented to students for evaluation should take into account the two sides of student participation – the creation, development, and end-product that is ultimately produced by the learner or their group, which is the VoiceThread itself, as well as the various comments made on other class members' VoiceThreads. As always, rubrics should be provided to learners beforehand so that they understand what will actually be assessed, and allowing them to ask questions about what is being assessed if they don't understand the rubric.

Evaluation rubrics, particularly those using indicators across several categories, are essential when assessing the quality of student work on any complex multimedia-based project. Although it is useful for the busy teacher to apply pre-made rubrics, it is even better if teachers formulate their own. Such rubrics can reflect their teaching environment and the points that they wish to assess. One good source for this is Rubistar, where there are a number of pre-made evaluation options as well as information on how to create unique context sensitive evaluation instruments. The rubrics section of the resources list also contains several other rubric creation tools that may prove worthwhile to look over.

Following are two sample rubrics that can be used with students in any classroom, including those participating in VoiceThread production from within the TESOL setting. One rubric focuses on the VoiceThread itself, in terms of student construction and development, and the other focuses on the student replies and comments to VoiceThreads created by their peers.

The rating scale used in the following rubrics go from 1 to 5, with 1 being poor, 2 fair, 3 average, 4 good, and 5 excellent. 'Average' is used as a midpoint so that students can see how each particular skill relates to peers. This allows teachers to identify those skills that are weak in individual students, and those that may need improvement.

VoiceThreads

Assessment Item	Assessment Criteria	Score
Media	Selection of artifacts reflects topic, helps support viewpoint of content (source credited where appropriate).	1 2 3 4 5
Content	Well researched and supported information relevant to topic is provided in an organized fashion (sources credited where appropriate).	1 2 3 4 5
Thread Quality	Images are clear, video is not blurry, volume is loud enough so that the voice of speakers is consistently audible.	1 2 3 4 5
Notation Tool	The tool is used to highlight when necessary, and is not used in a manner that is distracting.	1 2 3 4 5
Collaboration (if appropriate)	Students/groups divided workload fairly, and undertook VoiceThread completion cooperatively.	1 2 3 4 5
Language Skills	Language use contributes to topic clarity, style, and development (e.g., appropriate vocabulary selected, consistent spelling and grammar).	1 2 3 4 5

Ratings: 1 Poor 2 Fair 3 Average 4 Good 5 Excellent

Comments

Assessment Item	Assessment Criteria	Score
Focus	Comments are directed to topic, stay on topic, and are more than a few words.	1 2 3 4 5
Understanding	Comments show clear understanding of topic and others' comments.	1 2 3 4 5
Accuracy	Comments are accurate and contain no errors regarding the topic, and clearly reflect thought and preparation.	1 2 3 4 5
Notation Tool	The tool is used to highlight points, and not for its own sake.	1 2 3 4 5
Language Skills	No spelling or grammar inconsistency in text-based comments, spoken comments free of superfluous wording and are more spontaneous than scripted in appearance.	1 2 3 4 5

Ratings: 1 Poor 2 Fair 3 Average 4 Good 5 Excellent

How do I get started with VoiceThread development?

After registering with the VoiceThread website and having a contact list of students, you will need to create you first active VoiceThread for use with classes. Initially, select an issue that maintains a focus on obtaining the desired outcome of a lesson or topic. For example, you may simply want the VoiceThread to give a voice to students who don't speak out in the classroom, or you may want the VoiceThread to promote discussion of a topic, or even to have it act as a turn-taking slideshow to promote a dialog-based language activity, a story, or even a student generated narrative.

A good place to start with initial development would be preparing the necessary media or content for use in the VoiceThread before planning what comments to provide alongside the presented content. This step would also involve developing initial comments that are short (one to three sentences perhaps), as longer comments may discourage learners (particularly beginner second-language students) who may reconsider their ability to leave a comment. This would be followed by ordering content so that scaffolded learning can be provided in a teacher-directed manner, but in a way that still focuses on providing content that maintains a student-centered approach to the use and access content that is presented and contained within the VoiceThread. To be successful in this endeavor, it is important to focus on developing a VoiceThread based on well storyboarded material and comments that inspire learners to add media artifacts and respond to your and others' comments so that the VoiceThread can grow. Chapter 14 contains a guide and resource notes that can assist in any initial VoiceThread construction and implementation, and it is designed primarily for teacher use. A similar VoiceThread creation handout which is oriented more toward student use, along with associated resource notes, is also provided in the same chapter. The use of this handout in the classroom can also be extended with the VoiceThread comment reflection extension activity handout, which follows it in Chapter 14. The reflection/extension activity can be used to prompt student thinking on comments, or used in a follow-up lesson that centers around a discussion of the comments that students found users left on their VoiceThreads. In either case, the reflection handout should enable learners to record items of interest, factors that they agreed or disagreed with, things that changed their thinking, elements that challenged them, and, along with language learning outcomes (such as new vocabulary or expressions that they were able to employ or pickup), things that they learned from engaging in VoiceThread use.

How do I encourage the growth of a VoiceThread?

After creating an active VoiceThread, and providing a link or sending out invites to students, all VoiceThreads will need to be nurtured. Three ways to do this are illustrated by Ferriter (2010), and are related to the following elements: viewing and thinking about the VoiceThread, leaving a succinct spoken or written comment, and leaving an effective spoken or written comment that promotes future participation. Although these elements are necessary in any VoiceThread, some targeting is required for the teaching of English to speakers of other languages (TESOL) context as detailed in the following sections.

1. Viewing and thinking about the VoiceThread
Students will need to examine the content of the VoiceThread, listening to and reading each of the comments by previous users (if any). To encourage active listening, to promote writing skills, and to develop thinking skills while stimulating interactive

involvement in the language learning process, students should collect, connect, question, and express.

Collect

While viewing the VoiceThread for the first time, students should collect their thoughts about the information presented, particularly anything that is interesting or new to them (including vocabulary or expressions), and write down this information in point form.

Connect

It is important to emphasize that students should attempt to connect the incoming information from the VoiceThread and associated comments with preexisting schema, and that they should build upon their existing language skills.

Question

Students should be encouraged to ask questions about the VoiceThread that they are viewing. Is there anything that is confusing? Is there language or content that is unfamiliar?

Express

Students might need help with being creative with their language use. Support students in their judgments.

2. Leaving a succinct spoken or written comment

In the teaching of English to speakers of other languages (TESOL), it may be wise to provide students with a series of set phrases to get comments started, and setting a sentence or word limit for their responses. Almost any conversation starter expression could be used to help students leave comments, particularly those from students' current textbooks. Even some idiomatic expressions can also be introduced – for example:

I remember a time …
I once heard …
On the other hand …
I wouldn't be caught …

3. Leaving an effective spoken or written comment

Learners of any sort, and perhaps even teachers too, might also need some general advice regarding commenting and responding. This is especially true if the comments are to promote critical thinking, new language use, and promote further participation and interactivity.

Repeat/rephrase

Restate part of a previous comment or the content that garners attention.

Detail

Put thoughts into words or text as concisely as possible. What exactly are you students thinking?

Elaborate

Make an exact point, or complete the language learning objective, while attempting to use new expressions or vocabulary gained from the VoiceThread.

Create

Spur the thinking of future commenters by providing a memorable finish to comments. One strategy may be ending comments with a rhetorical question or by leaving a quote as a summary. Comments need to be closed in a manner that helps to spur conversation.

It is important to ensure that students are prepared to have other people respond to their comments in both a negative and positive manner. If learners receive a negative response, they first and foremost need to accept the criticism and not be offended. Help them learn to use any response as an opportunity to gain feedback and an understanding of others' opinions and ideas, and as a means to improve upon their language skills. Second, ensure that students take the time to properly organize their thoughts so that they can respond to any comments in a constructive manner. Time to compose responses is one of the biggest advantages afforded by asynchronous communication. Also, as the internet and VoiceThreads are potentially open to the public, and can remain a matter of public record until the VoiceThread owner deletes the thread, you should ensure that students are responding appropriately and in ways conducive to their language learning.

How would I create and house a VoiceThread?

Like many software tools and web sites, the VoiceThread website works by stepping users through a wizard so that a VoiceThread can be created simply in only a few steps. However, before you can start creating a VoiceThread and before your students can start commenting and creating as well, you first have to register with the website. It's free, and it creates an account specific to you to house the VoiceThreads that you create, and it gives you quick access to the VoiceThreads that you have subscribed to. This walkthrough explains the process through use of the VoiceThread website which is accessible via an internet-based browser. The process using the Android or iOS-based application is similar.

Step One – Starting out:
Signing in

Go to the VoiceThread website, then click on either 'Sign in' or 'Register'. If you are a new user, you will have to sign in, after which you'll then see the basic account navigation page. Other paid account options, with their own special features, are also available (K-12, Higher Ed, Business, and PRO), but these won't be discussed here.

Step Two – Navigating:
The welcome page

The most important tabs on the initial navigation page are 'Browse', 'Create', and 'Home'. Clicking the 'Browse' tab will bring up all the VoiceThreads that authors have chosen to be available for browsing. After you create a VoiceThread, you will be given the option to include it under this section, or you may wish to disclude it for increased privacy, particularly if you are creating VoiceThreads with students and are not paying for one of the educational platforms available. The 'Create' tab is the place to start when wanting to make a new VoiceThread, after which you will find the created thread housed under the initial page that greets you after log in – the 'Home' screen. This section presents you with a thumbnail view of all the VoiceThreads that you have created, ones that you've been invited to view, and others that you have chosen to subscribe to. Any small yellow quote bubble over a VoiceThread indicates that the thread has unread comments.

Step Three – Creating your VoiceThread:
Uploading content

To begin, click on the 'Create' tab from the main page after signing into your VoiceThread account, then click on the 'Add media' button or drag and drop files into the browser window for upload. You will then be able to upload a variety of media artifacts from a number of sources, but do keep in mind that single file sizes are limited to 25 MB for free accounts and 100 MB for paid accounts. Media choices may include pre-prepared documents (DOC, DOCX, ODS, ODT, PDF, XLS, XLSX), graphics (BMP, GIF, JPEG, PNG), presentation files (ODP, PDF, PPT, PPTX), movie files (AVI, FLV, quicktime, WMV – depending on the codec, with H.264 preferred), or with paid accounts sound files such as MP3 or WAV format for uploading prerecorded comments. Source options for media files include uploading directly from your computer, selecting sources by URL (uniform resource locator, or web page address), recording direct from your webcam or from a number of other internet-based services. These other internet-based services include: accessing any images from VoiceThreads appearing on your 'Home' screen, grabbing photos from your Flickr account, accessing photos from your FaceBook account, as well as providing access to the Khan Academy and free images available from the New York Public Library. Essentially, any number of items can be imported into a single VoiceThread, and you can always return to a VoiceThread to add more items or more slides, or even come back to rearrange the content that has already been imported. Just remember, when using a free account, you will be limited to creating only three VoiceThreads, but of course these can be deleted and new ones created as necessary, or you may even choose to export them (for a fee). Of note, formats that will not be accepted at all for upload include: HTML, SWF, TXT, and ZIP.

Step Four – Marking up the VoiceThread:
Leaving comments

The process of commenting is the same for any registered user, from teachers and students to the general public. To leave a comment on your VoiceThread, or any VoiceThread for that matter, first select the slide that you want to make a comment on by clicking on the left or right arrows to navigate to the slide you want. Alternatively, you can click on the 'Slide' button to bring up a thumbnail view of each slide in the VoiceThread, and click directly on the image of the slide that you want to leave a comment upon. Once you are at the slide that you wish to comment on, several commenting options become available on the comment panel after clicking the 'Comment' button. You can record a voice comment by telephone, or record a video comment using your web camera. You can also record a voice comment by microphone, or simply type a text-based comment with your keyboard. A prerecorded mp3 or wav file can be uploaded, but only if you have access to a paid account. After making a comment, it can be previewed before being saved on the VoiceThread slide. In addition, a notation function is available when recording a comment. The notation function provides access to a pen that allows doodling over the slide, and is controlled by the mouse. The color of the notation can be changed from the default white if desired, and can be rendered brighter or duller as necessary. Each time that you leave a comment on a VoiceThread, a thumbnail of your personal icon will appear to the left or right side of that particular slide. People will then be able to interact with your comment by clicking on your image. Underneath the VoiceThread is a comment line that graphically illustrates the length of the time each comment will take to play, and this can also be used to navigate amongst comments and play them back in any order, rather than letting them play sequentially.

Step Five – Publishing your VoiceThread:
Sharing options

Publishing your VoiceThread involves setting viewing options, managing the distribution of the thread, and then obtaining a distributable link. Once you've uploaded the desired content to your VoiceThread and made any appropriate comments, you will be at the 'Share' stage. To ensure that your VoiceThread will be viewable by more people than just you, it is important to click on the 'Options' button. This step is also important for ethical reasons, as it is here that you can ensure that suitable choices are made regarding student privacy. Publishing options include: allowing anyone to view the thread, or only those designated (recommended for school age use); allow anyone to comment (recommended), or no comments accepted; allow comments to appear immediately, or approve comments before they are visible to others (recommended); and the VoiceThread is viewable by all in the 'Browse' section, or the VoiceThread will not appear in the 'Browse' section of the VoiceThread home page (recommended). You may of course decide on the options appropriate for your teaching context, but these suggestions would work for many educators. Just keep in mind that VoiceThreads that appear on the 'Browse' page are also viewable and indexed by other sites such as search engines like Google. After saving the publishing options, you can click on the 'Get a Link' button so that the VoiceThread Share URL can be copied to the computer's clipboard. The link can now be pasted into an email for distribution.

Step Six – VoiceThreading one step further:
Embedding, playing back, or exporting
  After creating your VoiceThread, and sending out a share URL by email or other means, you may also want to consider embedding the thread into the school learner management system (LMS) or your own personal website, fine-tuning playback options, or exporting the thread. After clicking the 'Options' button, playback can be refined in the following manner:

- by setting timing options (in seconds) before each slide moves on to the next (four or five seconds is recommended);

- start playing when opened (recommended);
- don't allow commenters to delete their own comments (not recommended); and
- allow others to export (not recommended).

Exporting is available by clicking the 'Export' tab after clicking 'Share'. It is an excellent feature if you wish to archive your VoiceThread along with the comments and notations made on it, or even if you just wish to share it in an offline context. A number of exports are allowed for those who have upgraded their account, but this is not the case for free accounts where a small fee is charged per exported VoiceThread. Embedding the VoiceThread, or to gain access to the code required to embed the VoiceThread, is available after clicking the 'Embed' button. The code can then be copied for use with your own personal site, or school LMS such as Moodle. Alternatively, the VoiceThread can be posted directly to notable social media sites, such as Facebook and Twitter.

Step Seven – Inviting users to comment: Setting permissions

Inviting users, or students, to comment on your VoiceThread is essential – particularly when teaching English to speakers of other languages. The VoiceThread link can be obtained by clicking 'Share', and to ensure others can comment on the VoiceThread, the 'Allow anyone to view' and 'Allow anyone to comment' options should be selected. Educators who can afford it may prefer opting for paid accounts as it can be a little easier in registering students and keeping them grouped under your own account and by classes, and also to work with VoiceThreads in a more secure environment. Nonetheless, for those educators who choose to provide a direct link to a VoiceThread, learners can then start to leave comments only after each has have registered as a user on the site.

Step Eight – Finalizing:
Finding your VoiceThread and turning it into reusable content

After you have created a VoiceThread, set up publishing options, and invited people to comment on it, you will then be able to gain access to it from the 'Home' screen after logging into VoiceThread. The 'Home' screen houses all the VoiceThreads that you have created, as well as others (such as ones that you have subscribed to). Each of the VoiceThreads has several options associated with it when you move your mouse over it. For all VoiceThreads, you can 'Share', or 'Remove' the VoiceThread, or identify how many views it has seen and how many comments have been left on it. Options for those that you have created include: 'Delete' to erase the thread, 'Make a copy' to duplicate the thread, 'Edit' to change the thread, or 'Share' to distribute the thread. The 'Make copy' function can prove invaluable as it allows you to duplicate the VoiceThread with 'Just your comments', with 'All comments', or with 'No comment' data at all. After duplicating the VoiceThread, and giving it a unique name, it is then open to further customization. You'll find it accessible from the 'Home' screen, and this method provides a fast and easy way to recreate content for different classes and levels of language learner, and provides a number of different options to begin to teach with VoiceThread.

What are the key points behind VoiceThread use in the TESOL context?

Several key points that need considering when VoiceThread technology is employed with language learning students include the following:

- Once created, VoiceThreads are immediately web-accessible. They can be embedded into other websites such as blogs, wikis, and of course learner management systems, and they can be used to provide extended learning.

- VoiceThreads are an online dependent technology. Contingency plans may be required to cover unexpected internet outage or technology breakdowns if they are being used with learners during class or work hours.
- VoiceThreads are extremely adaptable. They are useful for a multitude of purposes across a range of subject and curriculum areas, and they afford a number of opportunities to engage in online discussion while practicing speaking and writing skills asynchronously.
- Keep comments succinct. Longer comments (four or more sentences) may discourage language learners (depending on their level), and some might doubt their ability to give the kind of spoken or written comments expected by the teacher. Keep in mind that students will attempt to emulate the kind of comments that you make, and that second-language students may need to be provided with starter sentences before they are able to construct comprehensive comments.
- Become involved in student constructed VoiceThreads. Provide guidance, advice, structure, authority, and most importantly, monitor continued thread development.
- Enforce guidelines. Regulate student participation, establish a standard of quality, and hold students accountable for their online work.
- Spotlight student comments. Reinforce effective comments and highlight the areas where poor comments can be improved.
- Always safeguard students. Constantly monitor all student-created VoiceThreads for inappropriate content and comments. Protect the privacy of learners and obtain parental permission to use VoiceThreads with students if necessary.

- Address copyright, and cite resources. Any works cited or used as resources need to be mentioned in a reference list, and this can be housed in a word or pdf file that can be provided on the last slide of a VoiceThread. Keep in mind that students may also need to be taught about aspects of educational fair use as well as plagiarism.
- Evaluate with a comprehensive rubric. Take into account the two sides of student participation, with the creation, development, and end product on one side, which is the VoiceThread ultimately produced by the learner or their group, and the various comments individual students have made on other class members' VoiceThreads on the other side.

As an interactive tool that allows for collaborating, sharing, and commenting, VoiceThread has come to change the way that information can be presented, disseminated, and discussed online. Essentially, it has come to open up new possibilities that provide second-language learners and their teachers with a means to engage in visually-based asynchronous conversations in a multitude of ways, while promising to provide language learners with another way to share their voices and practice language output.

4. User-Generated Content: Blogs and Wikis

4. User-Generated Content: Blogs and Wikis

Overview

Blogs and wikis are different to other websites because they demand interaction. Blogs ask readers to think and respond to the various ideas, questions, and links that have been posted by the author or authors. Wikis demand interaction by inviting readers to contribute, edit, and author the content of the website. The emergence of blogs and wikis, as well as other user-generated content, has shifted the web from a place of 'static' information provision (Web 1.0) to one of 'dynamic' information sharing and user-generated content (Web 2.0), and it is these elements that lie at the heart of the social media movement. People blog so that their voices and thoughts can be heard, and they create and edit wikis so that their knowledge can be shared. Bloggers interact with readers by providing links within their posts, and by responding to reader comments on their posts. Meanwhile, there are three categories of people accessing a wiki: readers, writers, and editors, and a person could be either one, two or all three of these.

Throughout this chapter, the manner in which blogs and wikis are developed is considered while taking into account their pedagogical promise when teaching English to speakers of other languages (TESOL). An overview of instructional strategies, tasks, and activities suitable for second-language learners of English when working with blogs and wikis is provided, along with the considerations necessary for applying these tools successfully in the classroom. Also included are tutorials, photocopiable checklists, handouts, and templates, evaluation techniques, and a comprehensive list of a wide variety of resources.

What are blogs and wikis?

Both blogs and wikis are a form of content management system (CMS), and they are similar in structure and logic with both providing asynchronous computer mediated communication (CMC) and operating through a web browser interface. A blog will contain articles that are usually written by a single author or blogger, and while visitors can add comments to the original blog post or entry, they are not able to change the originally posted content. A wiki, on the other hand, will contain a single piece of content that has potentially had multiple people working on it, with a single article having from one to perhaps ten or even hundreds of authors coming to form it. This editability and collaborative production are what differentiates blog posts from wiki articles. In either case, blog posts and wiki article edits, when they are made, are instantly visible to all other users.

Blogs

The term 'blog' was coined in 1999 (Merholz, 1999), and arose from splitting the term web log (coined in 1997) into 'we blog' (Wortham, 2007). Essentially, a blog is a web site where a user or a number of users post entries in journal style, and these appear in reverse chronological order. Writing to and updating a blog is easy and can be done from any web browser.

The first blogs were mainly journal or diary-based entries about a person and their day-to-day activities and thoughts. These days, blogs cover almost any topic imaginable, from those bloggers that talk about themselves and their daily lives, through to others who mention nothing about themselves but post articles that provide tips, technical information, scandals and rumors, or specific advice regarding their interests. This has led to many niche blogging sites on topics like health, cooking, gardening, diving, rock climbing, and flying. Niche sites also allow for guest bloggers to post articles on other bloggers' sites. Today, there are more than 100 million blogs in the blogosphere (the online community of blogs and bloggers) (Gunuelius, 2016).

Recent blog posts are very different from those that were made when blogs where new to the internet. Blog entries now contain multiple links, both to other blog entries by the same blogger(s) or to other sites. A wide variety of multimedia is also embedded into posts, from images and audio through to video. For this to occur, a number of sites have appeared that offer basic blogging templates (for example, WordPress) through to ones that rely exclusively on multimedia (for example, Glogster where each post is a multimedia-based poster). A number of other kinds of blogging also exist including vlogging (video blogging), and microblogging (for example, using Twitter or Tumblr). Perhaps the most famous site for blogging is Facebook.

Generally, though, all blogs hosted on their own website have a similar layout, contain an archive, a feed, and blogrolls, and require comment management. All blog posts are contained in a blog archive, and when an updated post is made, a really simple syndication (RSS) feed can be used to syndicate the entry and allow an aggregator to automatically collect the latest post for blog members to read. An RSS feed is a file that is used to subscribe to a place like a blog, podcast, or a website, and when those places are updated with new information, it is pushed to the aggregator. News aggregators are useful in that they utilize RSS to curate content automatically. This saves you checking all of your saved links for new information which may or may not be there, and allows you to see what is new – all in one place. A number of news aggregator applications and websites exist (for example, Feedly, Feed Wrangler, and Pulse). A blogroll contains all the links to other blogs or sites that are of interest to the blogger, or that are similar to the blog being read. A number of blog hosting sites offer a built-in link manager to generate this content.

Aside from these aspects, which are largely automated, managing comments is important for a blog. Comments can be the life of the blog, and offer direct involvement in a conversation with other commenters, or with the blog author(s) themselves. Comments also allow for features such as trackbacks (or pingbacks), which is a means of providing a link to a comment or article on another blog that your blog readers can then see and interact with. Monitoring systems are important as comment posts will also at some point receive spam, either from a person or a bot, and a visit from a troll.

Essentially, blogs are all about communication. A blog with a lot of content is generally going to reach a wider audience than one with only a few articles or links, or just static information. If content is regularly updated, this will ensure more comments and potentially more visitors. Visitors to the blog site will engage in some form of interaction with the blog when they visit, they will follow links to archived posts or other sites, watch videos, listen to audio, or leave a link or comment on an entry.

Wikis

A wiki is basically a dynamic web site where anyone can edit anything anytime they want using any web browser, and this operates on a principle of trust. Essentially a wiki is a server-side program that allows for collaboration in order to form the content of the site, allowing users to add, remove, or modify available content. They enable documents to be written collaboratively and quickly, hence the phrase 'wiki wiki' (meaning fast in Hawaiian) was coined (Leuf & Cunningham, 2002). This term was, in fact, originally used to refer to the first software to be called a wiki: Wiki Wiki Web, which was installed on the net in 1995, and this site is still visitable today.

A wiki can be thought of as a database that uses hypertext to keep track of entries and interlinked information to create a knowledge base. The term wiki can be used to refer to either a website, or to the software used to create the website. Any wiki allows users to change, edit, add, or reorganize content through a simplified browser-based web interface that has support for hyperlinks, the use of a simple syntax for the creation of new pages, and the formation of crosslinks between internal pages. It is not necessary to know any HTML (hypertext markup language). A user can review the history of changes, edits, and additions of the page that they are working on, or preview their changes before publishing them to the internet. Users can also use a sandbox for testing and experimenting with wiki syntax if they are just starting out. The simplest wiki program allows users to create and edit content, and more advanced wikis have management components that allow for a moderator to accept or reject any changes. Although wiki pages can be maliciously deleted, they can also be easily resurrected from a change history file. Those wiki pages that are bot maintained are also automatically regenerated if they are deleted.

There are also wiki farms where two or more wikis run on the same web server and share common components. They also offer a global search facility which can help when scanning through all the different individual wikis housed on such a site. Perhaps the most well-known wiki web site is Wikipedia.

Essentially, the concept of 'open editing' that wikis provide has had a profound and subtle effect on wiki use, encouraging democratic use of the internet and promoting content composition by any user regardless of technological savvy (Leuf & Cunningham, 2002). This means that a wiki article becomes the sum of knowledge of all the people who have contributed to shaping it, and acts as a group created database. It is for this reason that a wiki can potentially become an excellent source of knowledge.

Ultimately, wikis are all about community, and today, a wiki on almost any topic can be found from travel (for example, Wikitravel, a worldwide travel guide) to city specific wikis (for example, Auckland.Wiki). Wikis cover a diverse range of subjects that support many communities (for example, artists, collectors, writers), and so they are a useful means of being able to expand community involvement and develop interest in specific subjects or activities. People worldwide can work collaboratively on online documents to create a range of peer produced content.

How can I use blogs and wikis in the classroom?

Blogs are proving to be an effective and valuable technology tool for learners and instructors. They can be used to extend the classroom from beyond the confines of the school setting, and they can be worked on at any time and from almost any internet connected device. This feature also applies to wikis. Blogs and wikis can motivate learners who might not necessarily participate in the classroom, provide media literacy opportunities, become spaces for collaboration and discussion, and enable scaffolded learning to occur. Further, the open-ended functions of wikis lead not only to collaboration, but to the reconceptualization of the functions of authorship and readership. Learners, as readers, must take on the role of arbitrator, editor, monitor, and writer, and exposing them to the construction and maintenance of a wiki can lead them to critically analyze the shared space within which they will now have to read, write, and think.

Teachers are using blogs in many ways in the classroom context which include setting blogs as writing assignments and as a method for both them and their learners to track progress of projects and class work. Blogs can promote analytical and critical thinking, while developing a community (Yang, 2009). Blogs can also combine the best of solitary reflection, with the social interaction afforded by interactive comments (Yang & Chang, 2011). Blogs can also promote associational, creative, and intuitive thinking, and are a powerful medium for increasing access and exposure to quality information.

On the other hand, wikis are being used in the classroom particularly for collaborative-based projects and providing students with a means to produce content rather than consume it (McLoughlin & Lee, 2007). However, it should be noted here that students prefer to create knowledge and produce their own content to that of editing other students' work (Lund & Smordal, 2006). Nonetheless, the power behind wiki use is the ease of editing and content generation from a digitally shared workspace. Wikis allow students to create web pages, link these pages together, and edit their own or each others' work very easily. Class wikis can be used as group collaboration projects, with the whole class monitoring content and making necessary edits and revisions. This editorial control in the hands of students gives them a sense of ownership and responsibility regarding the site. Wiki use can also help students develop collaborative skills, learn how to publish, negotiate with others, and agree on correctness, meaning and relevance.

No matter what the task, blog and wiki use can help foster both communication and community in the classroom. A number of means of putting blogs and wikis to use would include assigning students to work in pairs or in groups to write and post summaries of content covered during class as a review task. Students could also be given tasks that involve fact checking of blog posts and wiki entries compared to a source such as their textbook. This would, however, this would need to occur with prudence in countries that are using 'revised' textbooks in schools. A series of blog posts or wiki entries could also be assigned on certain topics, or each student could be provided with their own blog or wiki page to maintain and which concerns a specific interest or issue. The assigned blog or wiki could then be used as a scrapbook or portfolio of files that is used to document work completed on a unit, any project work, books and articles read, or even posts and entries regarding highlights of class time. Book and movie reviews, trailers, and summaries could also be worked on collaboratively and then posted to blogs and wikis, with other groups of students reacting in comments or on forums. Blogs and wikis also offer themselves support for a number of projects like oral history reports, and for detailing a series of steps or instructions, along with the hosting of student-created podcasts and screencasts. Storytelling development can also be fostered with either students working on writing in a round to write one paragraph or sentence with another student following, or working together collaboratively to produce the entire story. Blogs and wikis are able to detail the contribution level of each student to a project, their responses to peers, and edits that they have made, and to serve to archive not only their submissions on an assignment or task but their responses to it and the effort they have put into developing it.

Blogs and wikis can then be used to showcase student work, and serve as an archive of submissions, before students post comments on other students' blogs and engage in the peer editing of others students' wiki content. Polls can also be used in conjunction with set blog and wiki tasks, topics, or assignments to survey students either for needs analysis purposes, or to determine student interest in the topic or their completion progress on an assignment.

Blogs and wikis are useful as organizers, and allow teachers to post learning objectives, assignments, and due dates, or even act as a place to post a weekly challenge such as riddle, with students posting potential solutions by the end of the week. Weekly summaries and reviews, teacher or student news, and classroom rules and codes of conduct could be hosted, along with notes and updates provided to students and other stakeholders on class events. PDF files of designated assignments, homework, worksheets, and handouts can be made available for download and archival purposes. Teachers can also provide links to students from a blog or wiki page that are much like those provided in WebQuests, and which are pre-screened and are able to provide specific and appropriate on-task information for students when using the internet or when working on a specifically assigned blog- or wiki-related task or activity. This is particularly important for young learners who can then begin to access internet-based content from a 'safe harbor' environment.

Every school district and educational institution has acceptable use policies in place regarding the use of the internet and computer networks, and these terms and conditions identify acceptable online access privileges and behavior. Policies regarding the display of any student work must be adhered to, and if specified, parental permission must be obtained before any student-generated content is published to a digitally shared collaborative workspace that is accessible by the general public. It is also important to ensure that each student is aware that there are limitations to the amount of personal and identifiable information that they should be publishing and sharing in a blog or wiki space.

Here are some of the pros and cons for blog and wiki use in the classroom.

- A fast and easy way to create a class website, but it takes time to update.
- Encourages participation that can then lead into classroom discussions, but it may prove difficult to keep students working on subjects that are relevant to class topics.
- An easy way to provide writing skills practice and improvement, but students may not write anything if they are not required to do so.
- Provides a place to collaborate on projects, but writing may be in a more casual style than that for formal submissions.
- A way to encourage shy students who don't talk in class to express themselves in other ways, but not necessarily quickly as it takes longer to compose, edit, and post content, or respond to it using a blog or wiki medium.
- A means of granting authorship which gives students a feeling of ownership, but which could create competition between students.
- Easy for all students to read and see each other's writing, but it may be difficult for some students to follow as communication is asynchronous.
- It is a public form of communication which encourages writing for an audience, but students may only write a

minimum if not required to do more with a set or directed task.

- They provide methods of sharing writing and ideas with people outside of the classroom, but this may mean a lack of confidentiality and privacy (although settings can be changed to adjust this).
- They can prove to provide an easy method for the instructor to digitally archive and collate student submissions and to assess levels of communication and collaboration, but they may meet resistance from those students who do not wish to use technology for learning.

What types of blogs and wikis exist?

There used to be a blog born every second (Keen, 2008), and now, this is every half-second, and today there is estimated to be 152,000,000 blogs on the internet (Gaille, 2013). Of course, not all of these blogs are active; some are abandoned, or lying dormant. Regardless, due to the sheer number of blogs that exist, there would be one for every subject area and topic imaginable, and they influence our decisions. They may help us decide on a product or which movie to see based on an individual review, or even change our lifestyle if we take action on suggestions made by a blogger presenting research on harmful or beneficial foods.

A number of blog types exist from so-called vanity projects that, despite being publicly accessible, are generally meant to be for an audience of friends and family, through to blogs that spread political messages, promote products, provide research data, give tutorials, and house podcasts and screencasts. Essentially there are three types of blogs: the personal (writing by one person about themselves and their day-to-day experiences), the corporate (providing updates about a company and personifying it), and specialist blogs (written by experts who provide insight into their specialization, or blog on it in terms of how it impacts or works in their lives). The specialist blogs in particular have come to see the internet turn into an easy-to-use database of information where specialists, like educationalists, put forward their thoughts and ideas, and build a discussion around them.

This is also reflective of wikis, which are built around a common community that shares their knowledge. The wiki then grows as people come together to edit it into an accurate knowledge base, and one that is reflective of the information and experiences that the authors, readers, and editors bring to it from their field of specialization. Unlike blogs, wikis are built with a sense of permanence (Godwin-Jones, 2003). Wikis that have been developed with this sense of permanence include those run by the Wikimedia Foundation (Wikipedia, Wiktionary, and Wikiquotes) through to cookbookwiki and fitnesswiki. Other categories for wikis, as Nations (2016) defines them, include entertainment, food and drink, game, health, political, product, and shopping, reference, religious, sports, and travel and geography.

"That's all very well," you may be saying, "but how do I locate the blogs and wikis that I'm looking for?" That's a good question. You can always begin with a Google search. You might also take a look at the 'List of wikis' on Wikipedia to find a wiki, and you can use the BlogSearchEngine or search RSS feeds using an aggregator when looking for blogs. They are out there, and they are easy to find.

What elements are behind effective blogs and wikis?

For blogs and wikis to be effective in the classroom, they need to be applied in ways that enhance student engagement in participative and collaborative learning. They also need to enhance students' multimodal literacy skills while providing them with a means of actively expressing themselves as they communicate on various topics and meet the six thinking levels of Bloom's revised digital taxonomy (creating, evaluating, analyzing, applying, understanding, and remembering) (Kent, 2015). For this to occur, it is important to regulate and structure student interaction with blogs and wikis so that content is produced edited and created according to desired learning objectives and, as James (2004) reminds us, giving control of the content to the learner. The role of the instructor then shifts, as Lamb (2004) states, to the setting up of problems that engage students as part of a learning community.

Establishing a classroom learning community is particularly valuable as it can change not only how students are taught but also how they experience the curriculum (Gablenick, MacGregor, Matthews & Smith, 1990), with shared knowledge, shared knowing, and shared responsibility at the heart (Tinto, 2003). This ties to Vygotskyian learning principles where knowledge is developed by interacting with other learners (especially the more knowledgable), through scaffolding, and through a zone of proximal development (ZPD) (Vygotsky, 1978). In this way, collective knowledge resides in the group rather than the individual (Nassaji & Cumming, 2000). Savery and Duffy highlight a number of instructional principles behind constructivist learning that can be applied to establish effective blog and wiki use with students, suggesting that teachers should:

- Provide reflective learning and practice by using authentic tasks;
- Include a number of taxonomies that encourage critical thinking, allowing students to provide their own solutions to problems;
- Create scenarios and set parameters that allow for problems to be solved;
- Provide a means for students to take ownership of the problem/learning; and
- Establish an environment where students are comfortable with making mistakes and are able to learn from making them.

Further, in terms of effective classroom assessment, blogs and wikis can be used for diagnostic, formative or summative assessment purposes. Diagnostic purposes may include asking students to post blog entries or create a wiki page concerning a topic before starting a new unit. Formative assessment may include providing ongoing feedback on a task or providing a summary of learning outcomes achieved from it. Summative assessment may involve blog and wiki use over the course of a semester or term, using it as an e-portfolio.

Ultimately, blogs and wikis encourage student interaction and collaboration in similar ways. Blogs and wikis also provide those learners reluctant, or unable, to speak up in a class an alternate avenue for their voice and a means to express themselves. Blogs encourage students to post articles, read and comment on other students' articles, and reflect on comments made on their own blog posts before considering if there is a need to post a response. Likewise, wikis encourage students to create articles to post, the reading and revising of other students' articles, and the need to reflect upon and review edits that other students have made to their own articles before deciding to keep those edits or not. The asynchronous nature of this kind of communication can prove advantageous here, as it provides learners with the time to think about what they are reading, and how they are going to respond.

How can blogs and wikis lend themselves to TESOL?

Finding the right one blogs and wikis to use in the classroom and in homework assignments, is important. They must not only be appropriate, but their use must also match with the topic and the assignment. Individual blogs and wikis on specific topics, over wikis that cover multiple topics in a general way (like Wikipedia), may prove more useful if using the sites as resources for assignments. Alternatively, a blog or a wiki could be started from scratch and either confined to the local network or posted on the internet, with learners developing all the content for it as part of any tasks set. In either case, and by their nature, blogs and wikis can provide an avenue for differentiation and the tailoring of instruction to meet student needs, and are perhaps viewed by many teachers of EFL and ESL as suitable for use in collaborative writing tasks. This is likely to be one of the most common ways that they are applied in the TESOL setting, but there are many other ways to use them in this context.

Any collaborative project is well suited to blog and wiki projects, providing a group activity where all students can be involved, and one where it is easy to see the evolution of student work and if they are working together equally (for example, by following individual blog posts and comments, or consulting the wiki article' change histories). As students write for a blog or wiki, they are consolidating their knowledge on a topic, and practicing and refining their reading and writing skills along with digital literacy and media literacy skills. As they write, edit, comment, and reply for a purpose, they are also creating ownership of the product that they are developing (Jatkowski Homuth & Piippo, 2012). While undertaking this process, peer-assessment and peer-editing also confirms for students that they are writing for an audience of at least their fellow students, and not just their teacher.

Campbell (2003) suggested that blogs be used as tutor, learner, or whole-class blogs, and in many ways, the uses that he sees for these can also be applied to wikis. Tutor blogs provide support for learning, links to various websites and resources including quizzes, and reminders about in-class tasks, all while encouraging learners to overcome their fears of reading in English and encouraging verbal exchange through comments. The learner blog could be run by individual students or by students working collaboratively in pairs or groups, predominantly in reading and writing classes where Campbell suggests that learners can post their thoughts on completed assignments and practice aspects of writing like journaling. The whole-class blog, which results from the collaborative effort of the entire class, can be applied with many different classes. In conversation classes it can be used as a bulletin board where learners can post messages, images, videos, and links related to classroom discussion, and it can be used to develop project-based language learning assignments that require research.

Horvath (2009), also sees blog use as a means of ensuring that the reading content for the course is student produced, with tasks set to take advantage of students developing and creating knowledge that they will need to complete future projects or tasks that are to be assigned later in the school term or semester.

In Saudi Arabia, Al Khateeb (2013) envisions the use of wikis in writing classes as aligning with tasks that arise from the use of the normal syllabuses, particularly when needing to develop the writing skills necessary for academic purposes. To this end, a blog or wiki could be applied to assist students in developing a process for writing, from a shared knowledge space, and using both cooperative means (working separately on pieces to create a whole) as well as collaborative means (working together to create the whole). However, Aydin and Yildiz (2014) found that wiki use with students in Turkey lead to various results depending on the collaborative task applied (argumentative, informative, or decision-making). The argumentative tasks prompted a higher rate of peer corrections, informative tasks yielded a higher rate of self-correction, and all tasks led students to focus more on meaning over form. Nevertheless, as a means of computer mediated communication, blogs and wikis can provide a variety of avenues for the use of task-based learning that incorporate authentic language and outcomes alongside support for student creativity. Mak and Coniam (2008) provide one such example from Hong Kong where incoming Year 7 high school students develop a wiki that illustrated the different facilities and features of the students' new school, which was then turned into a distributable brochure for their parents.

Blog post and wiki article topics can vary from review summaries of material and language points learned in class if the focus is largely on speaking and teaching conversation, or they can be used to write in a number of ways, such as essay style, if applied in the context of a writing class. Other blog and wiki uses may see students writing stories around a photograph, or using photographs as story starters. In this case, one student would post a photograph and the next would start to write the story, or a few sentences, before posting their own photograph for the next student again to continue the process. A wide variety of topics can suit such an activity, and it would lead to a diverse range of vocabulary and sentence structures being produced as all students complete the task. An alternative to this would be a student posting a short video of themselves speaking a sentence or two of a story, or thoughts on a topic, followed by a video by the next student who would continue the story or topic with one or two sentences, and so on. These kinds of labeling techniques encourage listening and speaking as well as writing and reading, and they can be extended to a wide variety of topics such as things to do with friends and favorite things (Yamauchi, 2008), or even to tasks that require responses to sentences like 'You won't believe what I saw on the way to school!'.

Students can also use blog and wiki spaces as common areas for collating information required for group work or other in-class assignments. They may be able to collect links to songs, and YouTube and Vimeo videos that are reflective of language points such as the grammar being studied in class, and house these links on their blogs or wikis with example sentences or phrases. A blog series or a wiki article like this can also be set from class to class, or semester to semester, with different student groups adding to it over time to create a study guide. Jatkowski Homuth and Piippo (2012) also remind us that blogs and wikis can be used for journaling, providing feedback to students, giving opportunities for peer editing, and the showcasing content in, say, a portfolio. Blog and wiki collaboration can also occur amongst different classes located in different locations or countries, particular between languages other than English (LOTE) and EFL or ESL classes, and this can lead to the development of posts and articles such as a day in the life of students in another class. Blogs and wikis can also be used as travelogs of class excursions, or used to develop a travel brochure to different locations or even to different time periods, if this suits a text being read in class or any unit or topic discussion that may have arisen during class time.

Other ways that blogs and wikis can be used may include the development and posting of a book trailer to a blog post after a wiki has been developed around the reading of the book, with a different page for each main character and chapter of the text. Books and movie review posts and articles can also be created in-class and hosted on a blog or a wiki when teaching a unit on movies. In turn, when teaching a unit on food, blog posts and wiki articles might reflect students' favorite recipes. Students can also be assigned to post new words that they have learned each week to a blog post, or to generate a list in a wiki article. This would lead to the development of a collaborative dictionary, built from the new words that students have met throughout the term or semester. This vocabulary could be used with flash card applications (for example, Memrise), and provide content that teachers can in turn use for in-class review quizzes in conjunction with student response systems (for example, Plickers). Blogs and wikis can also provide an avenue where students can ask questions about language, topics discussed in class, and even assignment completion with peers or the instructor responding. In turn, this can lead to the development of a class frequently asked questions (FAQ) page.

Blogs and wikis can also be used in conjunction with other technology including talking avatars. Voki is one example of a customizable talking avatar that can be embedded into a blog or wiki page for free. Technology like this can add a more human feel to the blog or wiki, and promote the opportunity of a higher level of engagement with the learning material. For second-language learners it can also provide another avenue for using their own voices. Talking avatars can also prove particularly useful when relying on blogs and wikis for presentations, and for students to practice listening to their own pronunciation as well as their peers' and their teacher's. The variety of engaging materials and the many add-ons that can be embedded into a blog or wiki can lead to both language practice and assist with core task development, and they should be explored.

It is also advisable, when working with blogs and wikis, to use a rubric and to set a minimum number for posts and comments, replies to comments, as well as the minimum number of sentences and paragraphs that constitute an article. In this way students will know how hard they need to work to edit or create their end product, and the expectations that they need to strive to meet.

How can I start using blogs and wikis with students?

Today's students may be considered digital natives (Prensky, 2001) but do not assume that this means that they will be able to use a blog or a wiki from the get go. As with any other technological tool or task applied in the classroom, students will need to be made familiar with and its application. Clear expectations both for learning goals and the use of blogs and wikis need to be established, with this then followed through with a means of engaging students in the learning process to ensure that they work collaboratively to meet goals, and that what they create can be adequately assessed and then showcased. To achieve this, clear guidelines, similar to those that follow, are essential, and would need to be established.

Guidelines for using blogs and wikis with students
One – Keep clear expectations
Develop learning outcomes or goals initially, and then work with the technology to ensure the task being set aligns with those goals or outcomes. Then, determine how best to assess the blog and wiki use – diagnostic, formative, or summative. Further, provide clear guidelines for collaboration, posting and

rewriting, as this will help students to maintain focus and stay on track, and it ensures that the mechanical aspects of any task can be met. It is vitally important to check school policy for social media use. Perhaps student photos are not allowed to be posted online at all, or they may require parents' permission or faces to be blurred. Students should be made aware that there are consequences for posting inappropriately, and written guidelines may be useful here.

Two – Develop over time

Keep a consistency with student blog and wiki work, and align this work with your expectations to ensure that students are reaching the goals set for achievement as they develop their blogs and wikis. If this is their first time, it may be better to start with a classroom blog or wiki that is developed slowly, with one assignment per week over a semester or term, or one that uses a single blog post or a single wiki page in one classroom session. If the choice for a classroom blog or wiki has been made, then it can also serve as a means of allowing archives of course worksheets and handouts, as well as a medium for updating students and other stakeholders (such as parents).

Three – Engage

Initially, engage students in the blog and wiki development process, either individually or as a class, by setting assignments that involve the use of a variety of blogs and wikis. Ideally, this can start out with students conducting assignments where they need to collect and then report on information gathered, and in turn store a synthesis of this information on a blog or wiki for presentation. Students could also be directed to collate materials for the development of multimedia blog and wiki posts, particularly by using sites such as Glogster. Reviewing other blog and wiki content can also inspire ideas to include on the classroom blog or wiki. As these tasks are introduced, it is important to demonstrate how to go about accomplishing them, so that students become familiar with the sites, and how to use them.

Four – Collaborate

The strengths arising from blog and wiki work are that they lend themselves easily to socio-constructivist models of teaching and learning, where learning is viewed as a process of peer interaction that is mediated and structured by the teacher (Jordan, Carlile & Stack, 2008). To this end, teachers can set specific tasks where students work as pairs or in groups to create their own blog posts or wiki pages on a topic in order to complete an assignment or to develop notes for a presentation. This would see students working around a teacher-directed theme to achieve specific learning goals while also being able to nominate who will take on certain roles and, when working on longer projects, if these roles will be swapped throughout a term. Students should also be reminded to preview anything that they work on before making a final blog post or wiki entry, and the teacher should ensure that they know how to revise their posts and edits if they wish to change these later. After the posts and edits have been made, encourage discussion of them while providing suggestions and on-going feedback.

Five – Assess

Any use of blogs or wikis for assessment must ensure that the tasks set for use with them aligns to the learning goals of the course, is reflective of course content, and is student-centered, with evaluation conducted by self, peer, or teacher. Consider also providing on-going feedback by commenting on student comments, their edits, and their posts as the course progresses. This will help students maintain a focus on their tasks, improve in areas where they may have been lacking, and see them brought back on track if necessary. Feedback and assessment for blogs and wikis, as for many other uses of technology in the classroom, needs to be ongoing rather than consist of a singular instance at the completion of a task (Al-Kilidar & Johnson, 2009). If making a blog or wiki from scratch, posting the assessment rubric to the site is worthwhile. Also, teachers, depending on the age range of students and the teaching context, may also consider having students help with the development of a rubric that is based on designated learning objectives.

Six – Showcase

At the end of the task, students work needs to be showcased. Casting a digital spotlight on student work is important because it reinforces the notion that the students are producers of knowledge and content and not just consumers of it. In this way too, blog and wiki work also begins to function as an e-portfolio, which comes to highlights student and class work as it is developed over a semester or term. Further, blogs and wikis can be used to showcase events, like field trips or classroom milestones, as well as student work and assignments. It is these blog posts and wiki pages that can then be spread across social media, like Facebook, with some stakeholders (either parents, or the students themselves) wanting to share these classroom achievements with others.

How do I evaluate blogs and wikis?

Perhaps the most appropriate means available to evaluate a blog or a wiki, particularly in the TESOL context, is to use a prefabricated rubric based upon a Likert-type rating scale. Any such rubric should be presented to students beforehand so that they can understand what will be assessed and expected from them.

Evaluation rubrics, particularly those using indicators across several categories, are essential when assessing the quality of student work on any complex multimedia-based project. Although it is useful for the busy teacher to apply pre-made rubrics, it is even better if teachers formulate ones of their own that reflect their teaching environment and the points that they wish to assess. One good source for this is Rubistar, where there are a number of pre-made evaluation options as well as information on how to create unique context sensitive evaluation instruments. The rubrics section of the resources list contains several other rubric creation tools that may prove worthwhile to look over.

An important point to consider when evaluating student-created blogs and wikis is that multi-literacy and penmanship in digital spaces is somewhat different to the pen and parchment process. The trick is being able to adequately assess aspects of student language use as they create their blog posts and wiki articles while also taking into account the comments and responses that they make on other students' blogs, and the processes that they engage in during wiki content creation and editing. In either case, it is important to take into account and evaluate both the avenue of communication and the content that results, and to this end, a sample rubric follows, and it can be applied equally when using either blogs or wikis. It has been crafted to work with both, as the 'group work' assessment item has been split into three levels of criteria ('overall', 'blog only', and 'wiki only') with each intended to be applied as appropriate.

The rating scale used in the following rubric goes from 1 to 5, with 1 being poor, 2 fair, 3 average, 4 good, and 5 excellent. 'Average' is used as a midpoint so that students can see how each particular skill relates to peers. This allows teachers to identify those skills that are weak in individual students, and those that may need improvement.

Assessment Item	Assessment Criteria	Score
Organization	Layout is appropriate (headings, keyword use, succinct titles, hook).	1 2 3 4 5
	Text flows, and has readability.	1 2 3 4 5
	Follows writing conventions: Structure (introduction, body, conclusion).	1 2 3 4 5
	Paragraph (topic sentence, support, concluding sentence).	1 2 3 4 5
Content	Meets learning objectives.	1 2 3 4 5
	Provides a significant contribution to the topic.	1 2 3 4 5
	Shows insight and understanding of the topic.	1 2 3 4 5
	Presents a balanced viewpoint.	1 2 3 4 5
	Free of errors, and plagiarism.	1 2 3 4 5
	Broad range of evidence, with claims sufficiently supported.	1 2 3 4 5
	Citations provided.	1 2 3 4 5
Technical	Links to internal and external websites provided.	1 2 3 4 5
	Links, and media relevant and connected to topic.	1 2 3 4 5
	No copyright infringement.	1 2 3 4 5
	Metadata is accurate, tags are appropriate, social media links and RSS feed are established.	1 2 3 4 5

Assessment Item		Assessment Criteria	Score
Language		Clear and concise, logical use of language, no confusing sections.	1 2 3 4 5
		Terminology used correctly, and explained.	1 2 3 4 5
		No misspellings or grammatical errors.	1 2 3 4 5
Group Work	*Overall*	Extensive edits and revisions made by all group members.	1 2 3 4 5
		Individuals contributed equally.	1 2 3 4 5
		Individuals fulfilled any additional assigned editing roles.	1 2 3 4 5
	Blog only	Each individual commented on at least one other groups post.	1 2 3 4 5
		Each individual replied to at least one comment on their groups post.	1 2 3 4 5
	Wiki only	Each individual made error changes to another groups article.	1 2 3 4 5
		Each individual added meaningful details to another groups article.	1 2 3 4 5
		Each individual provided additional evidence (media or links) to another groups article.	1 2 3 4 5

Ratings: 1 Poor 2 Fair 3 Average 4 Good 5 Excellent

What tools are available for blog and wiki creation?

There are many tools that are freely available and from which to select and begin blog and wiki creation. Once you have chosen a site or a tool, then setting up the blog or wiki is usually straightforward, especially if you have elected to use a free hosting service rather than self-host.

A number of free hosting sites allow you to customize your blog or wiki by editing the code of the templates on offer, or by allowing you to import templates that you may have obtained from elsewhere. Most sites and tools also allow you to import a range of media elements to further personalize your digital space.

Some of the most popular online utilities to support blog and wiki creation are:

Blogs

Blogger.com will host your blog for free, and aside from being simple to use, it allows some level of privacy which makes it suitable for use as a class blogging site. From one account, you can create as many blogs as you wish, and determine who is allowed to comment on the content.

Edublogs.org allows teachers to create and mange their own and their students' websites. There is room for customization of design and the ability to add various media to this private and secure platform.

Kidblog.org is an easy-to-use safe, and secure publishing platform designed for students in grades K-12. There are a number of excellent features including privacy, password protection, no need for student personal information to be collected, and no advertising. It is free for up to fifty students per class.

WordPress.org is one of the most popular blogging platforms in use today as it is open source, and is easily customizable. The downloadable software for self-hosting purposes is much more flexible than what is available on the blogging platform.

MicroBlogging

Twitter deserves a mention here as it is useful for microblogging (posting short frequent updates). It allows users to post and read short 140-character posts called tweets.

Tumblr is a blogging platform open to those over thirteen years of age, with most users using pen names. Users can post on their blog, follow others, and search posts. It is unique in that posts are divided into media types: text, photo, quote, link, chat, audio, and video.

Wikis

PBworks (formerly PBwiki) is a real-time collaborative editing system with several solutions including one for educators. It offers a single workspace where student accounts can be created without email addresses, and easy editing without the need for coding.

PmWiki is a wiki tool that gives user access control over individual pages, so they can be set for access by specific people, and to have different passwords for each page. The software also allows for navigation trails through individual sections, insertion of tables, and a printable layout.

Wikidot offers members the ability to create a wiki-based website with forums, and they can create a community, and publish and share documents and content.

Wikispaces is a free wiki hosting service that provides educators with a means to monitor student progress in real time, the ability to easily create projects and assign them to students, editing tools, the means to monitor student progress in real time, and a social newsfeed.

How do I establish the use of a blog or wiki in the classroom?

When looking to establish the use of blogs or wikis in the classroom, several factors need to be considered, and these are outlined in the following steps.

Step One – The approach

Whether blogging or using a wiki, the path taken will always needs to start with a plan. Decide what the blog or wiki will be about, what students will do in the digital space, and if media will play a central role in the completion of tasks. For example, will students take photographs and video, or record audio? Will they write posts or construct articles around these media artifacts, such as describing events, telling a story, developing a podcast or screencast, or providing a virtual tour? Set the focus and approach to encourage students to create content that they are willing to share and that other students would be willing to read and link to. You should then be able to justify any blog or wiki use in terms of how it assists in the language learning process, and be ready to provide this rationale to various stakeholders (including parents, administration, and the students themselves). Finally, ensure that your plan matches with any policies set in place by your school. With all of this done, the next step involves selecting a tool.

Step Two – The tool

The right blog or wiki tool to use depends on the teaching and learning context that you find yourself working in, and a number of appropriate tools for use in the educational context have already been discussed. Yet, no matter the tool chosen, restrictions need to be set. Choices need to be made as to who can see posts and edit them, who can post articles and edit them, who can post comments and reply to them, and who may revert a wiki site to an earlier version. Other matters that need considering are the parts of the blog or wiki that are important to protect or lock from changes as well as the sections that may need moderating for appropriateness, and who is to be responsible for carrying out this task (teacher or student). It also needs to be decided if the site will be locally or externally hosted, and who will be able to join the site and view it. Once these decisions have been made, arrange access to the site for students, and ensure that all of them are able to register successfully. This also means ensuring closure of the digital divide (Mossberger, Tolbert & Stansbury, 2003), and any students who cannot access the blog or wiki at home or from a smartphone will need to be provided with access at school or some other alternative. Further, be prepared to reevaluate the appropriateness of the tool as students use it.

Step Three – Setting tasks

Decide on the kinds of tasks that the blog and wiki will be used for, and how these sit within your curriculum (or the associated topic) and your students' levels, and consider any methods of assessment that may be required, be they diagnostic, formative, or summative. Be consistent with the use of the blog or wiki: once a week in-class or for homework over a term; or once a month used as part of a review task. Above all, moderate student work to ensure that they remain on track and are posting and editing appropriately. Setting guidelines and handouts to assist them in this process will prove useful. In addition to having standard member roles for any tasks, it may be beneficial to assign specific group members to certain roles, or get students to assign these extra roles themselves (for example, post/article editor, citation editor, chief editor). The photocopiable section of this book contains several handouts for these purposes. A further point of note here is that inaccurate content or writing during task development can be used as learning opportunities about things like plagiarism, copyright, or language learning points.

Step Four – Content editing

After setting up a blog or wiki, students will either need to make a new post or create an article that can be edited, and each blog or wiki tool will be slightly different to use. However, creating a new blog post is often similar to typing an email in a web-based email client (for example, that provided by Gmail). All posts can be previewed before being posted, and edited by the post author(s) once they have been posted. Leaving or replying to a comment is as simple as typing into the comment box and clicking a button such as 'Publish'. Almost all wiki software contains a 'Sandbox' where students will be able to play with the development of the wiki. Most wikis can be edited after clicking on a link such as 'Edit page', from where you can then enter and edit text. Some wiki coding may be required, and although not the same, it is very similar to HTML. A change history is also kept alive in a wiki, and clicking on a link such as 'Page history' would allow you to see who has made previous edits to the wiki along with the changes made. The history list can be used to revert the page to any previous incarnation as necessary. Each wiki page also has a commenting section that students can use to plan out their wiki page as they work, and the teacher can use it to provide encouragement and feedback on the task. To ensure that students stay on task when posting, commenting, replying, editing, and creating content, it may be necessary to develop handouts or use existing ones; for example, the format expected for blog posts, or a checklist for how to engage in editing an article on a wiki. Several handouts like these are available under the photocpiable section of this book.

Step Five – Sharing and assessing

Generate traffic to the blog or wiki. Visitors can be other students, or stakeholders such as parents. Ensure that site feeds have been established so that you do not have to continually check pages, but can use an aggregator to see when students are updating blog posts or editing wiki articles. Many wikis can also be set to email changes as students make them (as a daily or weekly digest rather than singular edits). Also, encourage students to provide readers with a reason to want to bookmark or share the blog post or wiki article; it needs to be creative or informative, and have social media buttons easily accessible. It is also important for students to have access to the RSS feed as this also informs them when peers have made posts and article edits. It also helps them to become familiar with the establishment of a personal learning environment (PLE), something recognized as important for 21st century learners and workers (Kent, 2016). Once the blog posts or wiki articles have been assessed and are ready for showcasing, it would be prudent to close the blog or wiki to revisions so that no further changes to the content can be made.

Step Six – Keep in mind
Define goals
Ensure that you have a focus from the start, both for the individual tasks set and for the overall rationale of using blogs and wikis in the first place.

Be consistent
Set tasks to use the blog and wiki regularly, especially if it is being used over the course of a semester or term.

Seek help
Provide avenues for students to ask for help when they need it, either from peers or from the teacher. You as the teacher should look for help if you need assistance with implementation.

Share
Provide social media buttons so that the post or article is easy to share, and encourage posts and articles to be written in creative and informative ways to encourage a desire in readers to share them.

Readability
Use bullet points, sub-headings, and bold and italic text to create posts and articles that are easily readable and well formatted.

Evolve
Technology is constantly changing, but with a background in blogs and wikis from this book providing key elements and a core of understanding that you can work from, it should be easy to keep up to date with any changes and what this may mean for developing blog and wiki use with students in the future.

Checklist

Use existing or fabricated checklists with students when they work to create posts and articles, and for when it is time for students to respond to, edit, or assess peer blog posts and wiki articles.

How would I use a tool to work with a blog and a wiki?

There are a large number of easy to use websites that provide blog and wiki hosting to educators for free, along with a number of tutorials on how to best use the sites. Alternatively, open-source software can be downloaded and set up to run from a local server. No matter the choice, both blogs and wikis are designed to offer visitors a means of interaction with the content, while plugins, modules, and widgets are able to expand the base functionality of the sites.

When using freely available blog and wiki services from any hosting provider, it is important to make decisions concerning usernames and who can view and edit posted content. Although both blog and wiki platforms are designed to allow any user to be a consumer and producer of content, it is not always prudent to use these tools with students, especially very young learners, and this may warrant a need to operate a closed blog or wiki. If operating an open blog or wiki, you may want to encourage students to use pseudonyms, and also decide if outsiders are able to make comments, reply to comments, or edit. Constant moderating of blog and wiki comments, as well as edits, would then be essential, and in this way, students can be protected from outside users who might begin to act inappropriately or irresponsibly. Once aspects like these have all been taken into account, the blog or wiki process can be initiated in a way that provides a range of learning opportunities for students and a world of varied instructional possibilities for teachers.

Please keep in mind that, although tools and websites do at times change the features that they offer and the layout of the interface, and may even become defunct, the following guides on getting started have been written in a way that any such changes will not impact on understanding the essential mechanisms behind the creation of a blog or wiki.

Working with a blog

Preparation
Before establishing a blog for use with students, it may be worthwhile to review several of those that are available across the internet so that you can get an idea of how other teachers are using their blogs with their classes. One of the most popular blogging portals is WordPress which is available in a multitude of languages. It could prove a good option to choose for a blogging platform as it can either be used online by selecting a plan from a number of options, or by downloading the open-source application for a local install.

Step One – Getting started
To begin working with Word Press for blogging, head to their website and click 'Register'. Each time after that, click on 'Log in', enter your username and password, then click 'Log in'. You will then be able to enter the URL for your first site, and you can create as many sites as you would like. The 'My sites' link will take you to your sites, and allow you to switch between the sites under your account. The 'Reader' tab allows you to follow the sites to which you have subscribed. Clicking 'Update your profile' will allow you to change your 'Public display name' to a pseudonym, and to enter information about yourself and the

sites in which your profile will appear. 'Account settings' can be used to change your 'Username', 'Email address', 'Primary site', and the 'Web address shown publicly' when posting, and 'Language' settings. You can also 'Manage purchases', adjust 'Security', and set 'Notifications' concerning new comments and likes on blog posts, 'Get apps' to manage WordPress sites across all devices, and take some 'Next steps' to alter the 'Theme' and 'Plan', to 'Start your first post', or to 'Create a page' such as an about us or contact us page.

Step Two – Customization

With a free WordPress plan, there are some customization options but some are reserved for those with a paid plan. Customization options include changing the way the blog looks and feels by being able to set a logo and tag line as well as a title, choosing a color palette for a background, changing fonts and header images, and changing the locations of menus. You are also able to change the nature of how a blog post displays by choosing between a full post or displaying an excerpt for the blog and archive pages, displaying an author bio on single posts, and choosing to display the date, categories, and tags associated with the post. Widgets can also be customized, like those that can be placed on the sidebar. The options are large and they range from blog stats and archived posts through to a calendar and pages that are available on the site. It is also important to note that the blog front page can be made 'Static' or it can be set to shoe 'Your latest posts'.

Step Three – Sites and page options

Click on 'My sites', then choose which of your sites that you want to work with, and you will be taken to that site's administration page. Here you can see the blog 'Stats' which include posting activity and post summaries. The 'Plan' option displays your current plan and allows for an upgrade if desired, the publish section offers a means to add 'Blog posts' and 'Pages', the personalize section offers a means to customize 'Themes' and 'Menus', and the configure section provides a means for 'Sharing' on social media and add 'People' to the site as 'Followers' or as 'Email followers' and assign them various roles such as 'Administrator', 'Editor', 'Author', Contributor', and 'Subscriber'. This is useful for adding students to a particular site's team, and assigning them different roles. Plugins and domain names can be added from here, and settings can be changed in 'Site profile', 'Privacy' (public, hidden, or private), 'Footer credit', 'Related posts', 'Change site address', are other options that are offered. There is also 'Start over' and 'Delete site'. The final option in the configure setting is 'WP admin' and this will take you to the WordPress 'Dashboard'.

Step Four – The dashboard

The WordPress dashboard offers an easy way to control all the behind-the-scene details concerning the management of your site, and it contains several modules that include: 'At a glance' (a count of total posts, pages, and comments, spam caught, and storage space), 'Quick draft' (a mini-post editor that can be used to post content or create a draft), 'Activity' (all the recent activity with options to approve or unapprove, reply, edit, see the history, mark as spam, and trash items), 'Your stuff' (your recent activity), 'What's hot' (the top and latest posts and news across WordPress.com), and 'Stats' (a graph of blog traffic and links to popular areas of your blog). The display of these items can be toggled on or off, and the display order can be changed. Also available is a navigation menu that provides links to all of the WordPress administration screens for 'Posts', the 'Media' library, 'Pages', 'Comments', 'Feedback' options, 'Appearance' options, 'Users', 'Tools', and 'Settings'.

Step Five – Creating and editing a page

You can create pages by clicking 'Pages' then 'Add new' from the dashboard, or by clicking 'Add' next to pages on the administration page. The pages added to the blog would provide readers with information 'About the blog' or with a means to 'Contact' the author of the blog. Once you have clicked 'Add', you will be taken to a what-you-see-is-what-you-get (WYSIWIG) editor which allows you to work with text and embed various media into the post. You can then add a 'Title' for the page and start to edit the content as you would in a normal word processing program. As you edit, a draft will be saved, or you can click 'Save' if you need to come back to the content later. You can set a 'Featured image' for the page and 'Preview' the edits, set 'Page attributes', and show 'Sharing' and 'Like' buttons'. Other options include a 'SLUG' or a URL friendly post title, 'Write an excerpt', set a 'Location', 'Allow comments' and 'Allow pingbacks and trackbacks'. After you have completed the editing process and made selections for the page, you can then 'Preview' it and, if satisfied, 'Publish' it to the site. To edit these pages at a later date, click on 'Pages' on the administration page. You will then be able to 'View' and 'Edit' each page, or send a page to the 'Trash'.

Step Six - Creating and editing a blog post

You can create blog posts by clicking 'Posts' then 'Add new' from the dashboard, or by clicking 'Add' from the administration page. Once you have clicked 'Add', you will be taken to a what-you-see-is-what-you-get (WYSIWIG) editor. which will allow you to proceed as in Step Five. You can set 'Categories and tags' for your post, a 'Featured image', 'Show sharing buttons' and 'Show like a button'. The post format can also be adjusted from 'Standard' to 'Aside', 'Image', 'Video', 'Quote', or 'Link'. Other options include those in Step Five, after which you can 'Preview' and 'Publish'. As a blog post it will appear on your site's main page in reverse chronological order. To edit the post at a later date, click on 'Blog posts' on the administration page. You will then be presented with an excerpt of each post and the date they were published, and you can 'Edit', 'View', peruse the 'Stats' of any post, or send it to the 'Trash'. When you are happy with the post, you can go to the front page of your site to see how it looks, and if it still needs some work, you can click 'Edit' at the bottom of the post to update it. You can also add a comment at the bottom of the post, as we can see in the next step.

Step Seven – Creating and editing comments and replies

To leave a comment on a post, navigate to the post that you want to leave a comment on, and click 'Leave a comment'. You will then be able to type your comments in a text box, and have the option to be notified of 'New comments via email', as well as being able to change the profile being used to make the comment. Once you are happy with your comment, click 'Post comment'. The comment will then be posted, and you will have the option to 'Edit' it, 'Like' it, or even 'Reply' to it. Various media, including images and links, can be added to comments and replies as appropriate.

Working with a wiki

Preparation

Before getting started in creating a wiki, it might be prudent to review several other classroom wiki projects to see what other teachers are doing and what might be possible for your classes. PBworks, like other wikis, has a community of searchable wiki pages created by educationalists with wikis that provide professional development, facilitate teacher to teacher communication, or focus on content area teaching to various grade levels. A search through the directory and a browse through some of these sites, would be worthwhile.

Step One – Getting started

To begin working with PBWorks to create a wiki for student use, head to their website, then click on 'Get started', select 'EduHub', and choose the 'Free option'. The free service provides a single workspace for up to 100 users, classroom accounts, 2GB of storage, and a number of customizable options. At this point you will need to choose a name and URL for your wiki, and verify your account by email. Next, select the view settings for the wiki; 'Anyone' or 'Only people I invite'. Then move to your wiki workspace.

Step Two – Getting students on board

After setting up the wiki, you can add classroom accounts for students by clicking on 'Invite more people', then 'Create accounts for your students'. You can then choose the number of students and the permission level that they will have (editor, writer, reader). Names can then be added, with the wiki providing a username and password automatically, and all this can be printed as a list for distribution. All users can be found under the 'Users' tab where they can be viewed, deleted, have their passwords reset, and permissions changed.

Step Three – Workspace security

After students have been assigned their classroom accounts, it would be wise to set the workspace settings under 'Access controls'. Here you can chose who will be able to view the site, 'Disable commenting for readers', 'Let workspace users see the User tab', or 'Let people request access to view and edit the workspace'.

Step Four – Monitoring changes via really simple syndication

Depending on the project, students may make up to fifty changes to a single wiki page in a classroom session, and it is difficult for one teacher to keep track of these changes, especially if there are thirty or more students in a class. A simple way to do this is to enable a really simple syndication (RSS) feed for the wiki site. This can be done under 'Access controls' by clicking on 'Notifications & RSS', and by default the site will 'Allow users to access this workspace's RSS feed and 'Enable email notifications for this workspace'. The RSS feed can be used by any news aggregator, and will provide an easy method to skim all the changes that students have been making. A number of news aggregator options are detailed in the resources list.

Step Five – Customizing

At this point you will want to rename the site 'Title' under 'Basic settings' and provide a description, then set the 'Space's time' and 'Contact email'. Other options here include changing 'Colors', importing a 'Logo' (for premium users), and 'Export' of pages.

Step Six – The front page

The wiki front page is the first page a visitor will see when arriving at the site, so it may be useful to edit this content to reflect news, announcements, and anything else of interest to students and visitors. The front page, like all the other wiki pages, can be edited by clicking on the 'Edit' tab, which will bring up a what-you-see-is-what-you-get (WYSIWIG) editor where you can enter content. You can also insert links to other pages or rename the page from here. A box is also provided so that you can describe the changes that you have made and saved (by clicking the 'Save' button). Links to other wiki pages, web addresses, and files can be added by clicking on 'Insert a link to a new page'. There are options to 'Upload files', and 'Insert image from URL', and the editor provides various means of inserting media including 'Video', and using 'Plugins' such as those including 'Interactive Media' to add a 'Voki'.

Step Seven – Creating pages

After setting up the wiki welcome page, it is time to add content and pages to the site by clicking on the 'Create a page' link from which you can 'Name your page' and put it in a folder if necessary.

Step Eight – Pages and files

The 'Pages & Files' tab allows you to access specific pages which also appear in a navigation sidebar on the first page of the wiki. After naming the page, you will be taken to a WYSIWIG editor and you can start adding content. After saving the content, you can view the page and send a link to others to let them know about the changes and to get feedback. As with all pages on the wiki, you can use the sidebar menu to 'Share this page', Put this page in a folder', 'Add tags', 'Control access to this page', 'Copy this page', and 'Check for plagiarism'. The Navigator 'Options' button will allow you to delete or move pages as well as 'Add folders' and 'Upload files' as needed.

Step Nine – Commenting

After you have made edits and have clicked on the 'View' tab to see the page, you will also be able to make comments on the page in the 'Add a comment' box. They can be seen only by site users. But the settings can be changed to make them visible to all who visit the site. Teachers can add comments that provide feedback, remind students of deadlines, and provide encouragement. Students can also use the comment box to provide encouragement and feedback to each other, sharing resources, and communicating asynchronously on aspects of the topic and any edits that might still need to be made. If the settings are enabled, comments can be removed by clicking 'Delete', and a 'Reply' can be left.

Step Ten – Reverting pages

If a page happens to be deleted in error, or someone has maliciously changed the content, you can always revert the page to an earlier incarnation. To do so, click 'Page history', and this will take you to a page history log that lists all saves of the page in reverse chronological order. You can delete these revisions, 'Compare' them, or select a revision to revert back to.

What are the key points behind blog and wiki use in the TESOL context?

A number of key points emerge when thinking of using blogs and wikis about teaching English to speakers of other languages, and some of the most important include:

- Blogs and wikis are a form of asynchronous computer mediated communication (CMC) that revolves around information sharing.
- Blogs are predominantly about communication, and wikis are about community, but both allow for collaboration.
- Both blogs and wikis allow students to produce content rather than consume it, and to react to existing content and influence it.
- A number of different types of blogs and wikis exist today, and all are reflective of the information and experiences that the authors and editors bring to them from their field of specialization.
- By their nature, blogs and wikis can provide an avenue for differentiation and the tailoring of instruction to meet student needs

- Blogs and wikis can provide a variety of avenues for the use of task-based learning that incorporate authentic language use, learning outcomes, support for student creativity, and the development of personal learning environments.
- The strengths arising from blog and wiki work are that they lend themselves easily to socio-constructivist models of teaching and learning, where learning is viewed as a process of peer interaction that is mediated and structured by the teacher.
- It is important to regulate and structure student interaction with blogs and wikis so that content is produced, edited, and created according to desired learning objectives, and gives control of the content to the learner. The role of the instructor then shifts to be that of establishing contexts and setting up problems that engage students as part of a learning community.
- The editorial control offered by both blogs and wikis in the authorship process gives students a sense of ownership and responsibility to these sites and their content.
- Students prefer to create knowledge and produce their own content to that of editing others' work, but peer editing and assessment is still crucial. For example, critical thinking skills can be promoted while students learn how to evaluate their own drafts, and while they provide feedback to peers.
- Clear expectations both for learning goals and the use of blogs and wikis need to be established, and then followed through with a means of engaging students in the learning process, ensuring that they work collaboratively to meet goals, and that what they create can be adequately assessed and then showcased.

- The asynchronous nature of this kind of communication can prove advantageous, as it provides learners with the time to think about what they are reading and how they are going to respond, with the shared responsibility of task development reducing cognitive load while providing social support.
- In terms of effective classroom assessment, blogs and wikis can be used for diagnostic, formative, and summative assessment purposes. Diagnostic purposes can include asking students to post blog entries or create a wiki page concerning a topic before starting a new unit. Formative assessment can include providing ongoing feedback on a task or providing a summary of learning outcomes achieved from it. Summative assessment can involve blog and wiki use over the course of a semester or term, using it as an e-portfolio.
- It is important to evaluate and take into account both the avenue of communication and the content that results.
- Set a minimum numbers for posts, comments, replies to comments, and sentences and paragraphs that constitute an article, along with any rubric used in assessment. In this way, students will know how hard they need to work on editing or creating their end product, and the expectations that they need to meet.
- Once the blog posts or wiki articles have been assessed, close the blog or wiki to revisions so that no further changes to the content can be made.
- Be able to justify any blog or wiki use in terms of how it assists in the language learning process, and be ready to provide this rationale to various stakeholders (including parents, administration, and the students themselves).

5. Lesson Plan Guides, and Example Implementation

5. Lesson Plan Guides,
and Example Implementation

Provided here are lesson plan guides as well as examples for implementing WebQuests, VoiceThreads, blogs and wikis in the educational context. The guides are meant to assist in the understanding of how to develop a detailed lesson plan, and to help describe what each component and stage of a lesson may cover. The example implementations are intended to provide a use-case scenario detailing the techniques required to apply the use of WebQuests, VoiceThreads, blogs and wikis in real-world settings.

The content covered here includes:

General
- Lesson plan general guide

WebQuests
- Lesson plan guide for WebQuest integration
- Example implementation: WebQuest – Book trailers
- Example Implementation: WebQuest – Book trailers: Handouts

VoiceThreads
- Lesson plan guide for VoiceThreading in the classroom
- Example implementation: VoiceThread

Blogs and wikis
- Lesson plan guide for blogging
- Example implementation: Blogs
- Lesson plan guide for wikis
- Example implementation: Wikis

Lesson Plan General Guide	
Teaching Context	
Level of Proficiency and Maturity	Student language level (e.g. beginner, intermediate, advanced). Student age range (e.g. young learners, adults).
Lesson Length	Time allotted for the class (e.g. 35-45 minutes).
Lesson Topic	Major theme or focus of the lesson (e.g. numbers and time).
Objective	Lesson aim (e.g. to teach students how to tell the time and date accurately).
Outcomes	Learning outcomes (e.g. students will be able to read analog and digital timepieces).
Relevant Prior Learning	Anything that students need to know before starting work on this lesson's content (e.g. students need to have completed Chapter Two of the book, and have previously met language associated with appointments, calendars, and timekeeping).

Teacher Preparation	
Hardware	Types of computer or peripherals required (e.g. USB sticks, MP3 players).
Software	Name of software used (e.g. Photo Story 3, Microsoft Word).
Webpage Links	Hyperlink to web resources (e.g. www.google.com).
Additional Resources	Other necessary materials for the lesson (e.g. handouts, worksheets, textbooks).

Procedure			
Stage and Timing	Objective	Teacher	Students
Review Stage (if required, 5 minutes)	Focus of stage (e.g. encourage the use of previously acquired language).	Indicate what the teacher says and does in each stage of the lesson.	Provide expected examples of student behavior.
Warm-up Stage/Pre-Technology Use (10 minutes)	Focus of stage (e.g. introduce new concepts and language to students in a meaningful manner).	Indicate what the teacher says and does in each stage of the lesson.	Provide expected examples of student behavior.
Main Stage/ Technology-based Activity (20 minutes)	Focus of stage (e.g. allow students to utilize technology to become familiar with and apply the concepts and language content introduced in the lesson).	Indicate what the teacher says and does in each stage of the lesson.	Provide expected examples of student behavior.

Practice Stage (15 minutes)	Focus of stage (e.g. allow learners to utilize the skills and language that they are expected to acquire during the lesson in a practical way).	Indicate what the teacher says and does in each stage of the lesson.	Provide expected examples of student behavior.
Lesson Summation Stage/Post-Technology Activities (10 minutes)	Focus of stage (e.g. instructor reinforces the importance of language concepts and skills acquired, stating how they will be useful in future lessons).	Indicate what the teacher says and does in each stage of the lesson.	Provide expected examples of student behavior.

Further Considerations	
Follow-Up Activities	Prepare material that can be applied in a follow up class. Also, be ready with activities for students who complete their class work earlier than expected.
Contingency Plan(s)	Always prepare an alternate teaching scenario in case of any problems. For example, a sudden power outage, or a timetabling issue could make the assigned room unavailable.
Evaluation	Reflect on what worked well, and what did not, and how you might deliver the lesson differently or improve upon it when running it again.

Lesson Plan Guide for WebQuest Integration	
Teaching Context	
Level of Proficiency and Maturity	Upper Intermediate to advanced. Can be modified for younger learners or lower language levels.
Lesson Length	Five lessons (over a week). Homework completion components. Time allotted for each class: 50 minutes.
Lesson Topic	Variable, from integration with a novel through to a unit on entertainment or on movie reviews to other forms of presentation.
Objectives	1. Develop critical thinking skills. 2. Enhance communication skills by asking questions, expressing opinions, developing narratives, and writing for an audience. 3. Strengthen media literacy and digital literacy skills (use software, images, audio, video, and other media elements or components). 4. Advance reading and writing skills. 5. Develop presentation and pitching abilities.
Outcomes	1. Students will complete a WebQuest on book trailers (refer to the 'WebQuest example: Book trailers'). 2. Students will employ a range of media to complete their WebQuest task. 3. Students will show evidence of critical thinking, the ability to effectively evaluate and critique content, and use rubrics effectively.
Relevant Prior Learning	Students will need to be familiar with digital storytelling in order to develop a book trailer, and have read the associated novel in the target or first language.

Teacher Preparation	
Hardware	Computer or tablet, with internet access and microphone, camera, and scanner (if scanning student work) for each group. USB sticks, YouTube, or Google Drive for storage of the developed book trailer.
Software	Media player. Digital storytelling tools (Photo Story 3, iMovie, or WeVideo). Note-taking tools (Microsoft Word or Pages – as required).
Webpage Links	See the resources section of the 'WebQuest example: Book trailers'.
Additional Resources	See the handout section of the 'WebQuest example: Book trailers'.

Procedure – Day 1 of 5			
Stage and Timing	Objective	Teacher	Students
Review Stage (5 minutes)	Remind students of a novel that they have read for class or for leisure. Ask about what made it exciting and interesting for them. Start to introduce aspects of language that students can use when creating a book trailer for the novel.	Teacher directs questions to have students start brainstorming on a recent novel that they have read for class or for leisure.	Students briefly tell about their pet or their weekend in story format, using appropriate sequencers.
Warm-up Stage/Pre-Technology Use (15 minutes)	Introduce the WebQuest and book trailer concept.	Provide students with the WebQuest worksheets.	Students go through the WebQuest sections with the teacher.

Main Stage (20 minutes)	The WebQuest has been introduced and students will complete Steps one and two by the end of class.	The teacher guides students in the completion of Steps one and two of the WebQuest.	Students complete Steps one and two of the WebQuest along with the associated handouts.
Lesson Summation Stage/Post-Technology Activities (10 minutes)	Students should be reminded of the lesson's goals. Each of the objectives of Step one and of Step two of the WebQuest should have been completed.	Ensure students have completed Handouts one, two, and three. Provide feedback and advice on how the handouts have been completed.	Students should have completed Handouts one, two, and three by this stage of the lesson. These can be completed for homework if work is still required on them.

Procedure – Day 2 of 5			
Stage and Timing	**Objective**	**Teacher**	**Students**
Review Stage (5 minutes)	Remind students of the WebQuest goals and tasks. Ensure that all students have completed Steps one and two along with the associated handouts.	Ensure students are up to date with the task, and are ready to begin Step three.	Students should have completed all tasks, and they are ready to start Step three of the WebQuest.
Warm-up Stage/Pre-Technology Use (5 minutes)	Go through the steps required to complete a book trailer under step three of the WebQuest.	Ensure students understand the steps they need to perform by the end of class.	Students should be provided with the necessary handouts, and access to the technology required.

Main Stage (35 minutes)	Students use the handouts to brainstorm their script, develop their storyboard, collect media for book trailer development, and begin to produce their trailer.	Assist students in working on the development of their book trailer, and ensure that they are working through the resources and handouts effectively.	Students begin to work through Handout four, five, six, and seven to complete their book trailer and the required minimum production requirements.
Lesson Summation Stage/Post-Technology Activities (5 minutes)	Students should have been able to complete the storyboard for their trailer, and be at the media collection or trailer finalization stage of Step three.	Ensure students have started to successfully develop their trailer using the applications that they have chosen.	Students should have completed Handouts four, five, and six at a minimum.

Procedure – Day 3 of 5			
Stage and Timing	Objective	Teacher	Students
Review Stage (5 minutes)	Remind students that they will need to complete Step three of the WebQuest by the end of this lesson.	Ensure that students have completed Handouts four, five and six.	Students are able to produce their completed handouts.
Warm-up Stage/Pre-Technology Use (5 minutes)	Remind students of the storyboarding process and the requirements that need to be met.	Ensure students understand how to use the application to complete their trailer, and are familiar with the checklist requirements from Handout seven.	Students should prepare their media and get ready to use the application that they have chosen to create their book trailer.

Main Stage (35 minutes)	Students should be working on finalizing their book trailer according to the required checklist.	Assist students where necessary as they complete their book trailer.	Students will use their storyboard and collected media to finalize their book trailer.
Lesson Summation Stage/Post-Technology Activities (5 minutes)	Students should have been able to develop their book trailer in full.	Ensure that students have successfully developed their trailer, and have completed the final checklist of Step three, using handout seven.	Students will need to complete Step three of the WebQuest by this stage of the lesson. Otherwise, completion will need to be set as a homework task.

Procedure – Day 4 of 5			
Stage and Timing	**Objective**	**Teacher**	**Students**
Review Stage (5 minutes)	Students should have completed their book trailer, and be able to now start work on their presentation and pitch regarding it.	The teacher ensures that all trailers have been completed, and that students have them ready for playback to the class.	Students will need to download their book trailer to the class computer or have it ready to playback from an online source.
Warm-up Stage/Pre-Technology Use (5 minutes)	Introduce Steps four, five, and six of the WebQuest to students.	Guide students in completing work on their pitch to present their book trailer.	Students will need to use Handout eight to help them prepare their pitch.

Main Stage (25 minutes)	Students work together to prepare a short pitch to accompany the playback of their book trailer.	Assist students in completing their pitch. It should be concise, and they should aim to speak one sentence each.	Students successfully sequence their story, and record an appropriate narrative with teacher guidance.
Lesson Summation Stage/Post-Technology Activities (10 minutes)	Students should be ready to play back their book trailer, and present their pitch in the following class.	Ensure that students have completed their pitch and are ready to present it in the following class.	Students will be able to review their pitch, and practice it for homework before presenting it in class the following day.

Procedure – Day 5 of 5			
Stage and Timing	**Objective**	**Teacher**	**Students**
Review Stage (5 minutes)	Review the WebQuest components so far completed, and introduce the steps to be completed for the lesson.	Ensure that students understand the steps needed to be completed for the day, and distribute the necessary handouts.	Students prepare to evaluate and critique others work, as well as present and pitch their book trailer to the class.
Warm-up Stage/Pre-Technology Use (5 minutes)	Student groups are given a short-time to practice their pitch and prepare their book trailer for playback.	Ensure students are ready to present, and are ready to evaluate others using handout nine.	Students have their note cards ready and are reviewing for their pitch.

Main Stage (35 minutes)	Students play back their book trailer, pitch their presentation, evaluate other trailers, and write a critique on each.	Guide students to present and play back their trailer, and keep to the set time limit.	Students will use Handout nine to evaluate each book trailer, and Handout ten to critique each book trailer.
Lesson Summation Stage/Post-Technology Activities (5 minutes)	A class response system, like Plickers, should be used to take a vote for the best produced book trailer.	Distribute and scan Plicker cards, and reveal the vote to the class.	Students hold up their Plicker card to vote for the trailer that they believe to be the best.

Further Considerations	
Follow-Up Activities	The book trailers can be included in student portfolios for end of semester or end of term assessment. The book trailers can be used to inspire future students who take this class to read the novel.
Contingency Plan(s)	Several activity sheets for review of previous material should be prepared to allow those students who complete tasks to keep busy with language content. Alternatively, some off-line language games can be prepared to fill in the time if technological problems occur.
Evaluation	What are the biggest frustrations for implementation? Can these be remedied next time? What are the successes of the lesson? What did students get out of this activity? Can more language practice be provided?

Example Implementation:
WebQuest – Book Trailers

Introduction

The world of book publishing can be an exciting place, and this is where you and your team work – in the offices of one of the world's most famous book publishers. There is an upcoming book launch, and your boss needs an award winning book trailer.

Task

There is a book launch scheduled for next month, and the author needs a book trailer specifically developed for their book. You will work in a team to prepare a book trailer for the author.

You will need to:
1. Review several successful book trailers
2. Learn how to create a successful book trailer
3. Present and pitch your book trailer
4. Evaluate and critique other book trailers
5. Vote on the best book trailer to represent the book on launch day

Process

Step one – What is a book trailer?

Review existing book trailers:
1. Watch at least five different book trailers
2. List five things that you think make for a good book trailer
3. List five things that you think make for a bad book trailer

Step two – Creating a book trailer

Understand the process behind making a book trailer:

1. Identify the stages behind creating a book trailer
2. Select software to create a book trailer

Step three – Producing a book trailer

Create a unique book trailer by working through:

1. Brainstorming
2. Storyboarding
3. Script development
4. Media collection
5. Trailer finalization
6. A checklist

Step Four – Presenting a book trailer

In this step you will need to present and pitch your book trailer:

1. Play it – share your book trailer
2. Pitch it – 'sell' your book trailer

Step five: Evaluating and critiquing

In this step you will need to evaluate and critique peer' book trailers:

1. Evaluate – peers' book trailers
2. Write up – the good and the bad

Step six – Vote

In this step you will need to vote for the best trailer using a classroom response system:

1. Plickers – vote for the best book trailer

Resources

Step one

In this step you will use several web resources, and an in-class handout to view several book trailers, identify what makes a book trailer good or bad, and prepare a list of the good and bad aspects of a book trailer.

1. Go to Book Trailers for Readers (http://www.booktrailersforreaders.com/), and watch at least five different book trailers.

2. Then think about what makes the good trailers good and the bad trailers bad. How did they captivate you? Did the trailers make you really want to read those books? Think about these kinds of questions while you review the following web sites:
   a) Fantastic book trailers and the reasons why they're good (Najafi, 2013)
   b) Why most book trailers are awful and how yours can be different (Goins, 2016)
   c) Book trailers and using video for book marketing (Penn, 2015)
   d) What makes a good book trailer (JLG, 2016)

3. Finally, list five things that make for a good book trailer, and five things that make for a bad book trailer.
   a) Handout one – 'Book trailers: The good and the bad'

Step two

In this step, you will identify the various stages behind creating a book trailer, identify appropriate software to help you create a book trailer, and detail these aspects on the in-class handout.

1. Identify the stages behind a book trailer
   a) Book trailers for readers (Harclerode, n.d.)
   b) How to make a book trailer: 6 tips (Sambuchino, 2016)
   c) How to make a book trailer for free (that looks professional) (Natsil, 2015)
   d) 12 easy steps to the making of a book trailer (Croome, 2011)

2. Identify the software available to create a book trailer
   a) Spotlight on business: 4 elements of an awesome animoto book trailer (Schiller, 2015)
   b) Book trailers: 11 Steps to make your own (Penn, 2008)

3. Detail the steps that your group will follow when creating a book trailer, along with the applications available and what makes these good choices to use when producing a book trailer. Finally, decide upon an application that your group will use to produce a book trailer.
   a) Handout two – 'Book trailers: Steps to create a book trailer'
   b) Handout three – 'Book trailers: Applications to use'

Step three

Now you will produce your book trailer. You need to take into account script development, storyboarding, media collection, and trailer finalization before conducting a checklist to ensure that you have met the production criteria as set by your teacher.

1. *Brainstorming*

Prior to starting out, start thinking about the book. Who are the main characters in the book? How do you feel when you think about them? What is the mood of the book? How does this mood make you feel? What images come to mind when you feel this way? What is the plot of the book? What captured you about the plot the most? Why would someone want to read this book? How would you persuade them to read the book? How would you interest them in the book? What images or video could you use to engage or connect them to the book? What details from the book did you find to be the most exciting, interesting, and funny? What other details could make someone want to read the book?

a) Handout four – 'Book trailers: brainstorming'

2. *Script development*

You will need to develop a short narration for your book trailer, as well as think about any on-screen captions that you may want to use. You can use the blurb of the book to help you prepare a summary. Try to use vocabulary that will persuade the viewer to read the book, engage them in the story, and keep them interested until the end. Start by thinking of an interesting 'hook' or captivating question based on a plot point to draw in the viewer. Use the appropriate handout to write out your summary and any desired on-screen captions.

a) Handout five – 'Book trailers: Summary'

3. *Storyboard*

The summary that you use for narration, along with any captions that you want to include in your trailer, will need to match any images, music, or video clips that you may also want to use for your book trailer. You also need to see how long your book trailer will be, based on the recording of your summary and how long you think each image, music clip, or video clip will play for.

a) Handout six – 'Book trailers: Storyboard'

4. *Media collection*

You will need to find images, music clips, video clips, and other media to use in the development of your book trailer. Pay attention to copyright, and only use images, music clips, or video clips that are in the public domain or are usable when crediting the creator.

a) Images: Pics4Learning (Tech4Learning, 2016)

b) Music: Free music archive (FMA, 2016)

c) Video: Mazwai (Mazwai, 2016)

5. *Trailer finalization*

Use the application that you selected to produce and finalize your book trailer. Reviewing a tutorial on how to use the application to make a book trailer can help you get started and get finished much more quickly.

a) Book trailer tutorial using (Windows) Movie Maker (Lion, 2014)

b) How to create an Animoto book trailer (Doyle, 2015)

6. *Checklist*

Ensure that your group has met the minimum production, language use, and playback requirements as set by your teacher.

a) Handout Seven – 'Book trailers: Trailer finalization checklist'

Step four

This is where you will need to present your book trailer to the class, and it involves playing the book trailer, and then speaking about it. You need to pitch the trailer as being the best to represent the book on launch, and each group member must give at least one reason for this trailer to be chosen as the best.

1. Play it.
   a) Upload your video to a site such as YouTube for online sharing and playback, or
   b) Upload your video to a USB drive to play back locally

2. Pitch it.
   a) How to do a presentation in class (WikiHow, 2016)
   b) Handout eight – 'Book trailers: Pitch it!'

Step five

In this step, you need to evaluate and critique the book trailers produced by each class group. You should do this in two ways.

1. Use the rubric to help you think about the book trailers as you watch them, then complete the associated handout after each book trailer has completed playing.
   a) Handout nine – 'Book trailers: Book trailer evaluation rubric'

2. After watching all of the other groups' trailers and listening to their presentations, write one paragraphs identifying at least one good and one bad aspect of each trailer, and submit these to your teacher for review.
   a) Handout ten – 'Book trailers: Critique'

3. At the same time that you are doing all of this your teacher will evaluate your book trailer.
   a) Handout nine – 'Book trailers: Book trailer evaluation rubric'

Step six

Here, you will watch each trailer again, one by one, and then vote for the one that you think is the best. A classroom response system will be used by the teacher to gather the votes anonymously.

1. Playback.
    a) YouTube or USB
2. Voting.
    a) Plickers classroom response system (Plickers, 2016)

Evaluation

Any book can be used for this WebQuest. However, it would be best if it is a novel that students have been studying recently or, perhaps for older students, a popular movie that is based on a book.

1. The completed book trailer can be evaluated using:
    a) Handout nine – 'Book trailers: Book trailer evaluation rubric'.
2. The completed WebQuest can be evaluated using:
    a) Handout eleven – 'Book trailers: WebQuest evaluation rubric'.

Conclusion

Students

1. Each group of students completes and presents a book trailer to the class as a group, and pitches why it is the best one for the author to use for their book.
2. Students write a one-paragraph critique of each book trailer, including their own, and are able to identify what makes for good and bad book trailers. The paragraph is submitted as a writing sample for the teacher to review.

3. Students use a rubric to identify the best class-produced book trailer, and the one that they think would be best used to sell the book.

Teacher

1. The teacher closes the WebQuest with a summary of the topic and the goals achieved by the students throughout its completion.
2. The best book trailer, as voted by the class, is identified.
3. The entire WebQuest is assessed the teacher
    a) Handout eleven: 'Book trailers – WebQuest evaluation rubric'

Example Implementation:
WebQuest – Book Trailers: Handouts

1. The good and the bad
2. Steps to crete a book trailer
3. Applications to use
4. Brainstorming
5. Summary
6. Storyboarding
7. Trailer finalization checklist
8. Pitch it!
9. Book trailer evaluation rubric
10. Critique
11. WebQuest evalution rubric

1. Book Trailers: The Good and the Bad

Group Members

Good book trailers ...

1. _____

_____

_____

2. _____

_____

3. _____

_____

_____

4. _____

_____

5. _____

_____

Bad book trailers ...

1. _____

_____

2. _____

_____

3. _____

_____

4. _____

_____

5. _____

_____

2. Book Trailers: Steps to Create a Book Trailer

Group Members

Steps to Create a Book Trailer

Step 1. _____
Description _____
_____
_____
_____

Step 2. _____
Description _____
_____
_____
_____

Step 3. _____
Description _____
_____
_____
_____

Step 4. _____
Description _____
_____
_____
_____

Step 5. _____
Description _____
_____
_____
_____

(Add more steps if you need them).

3. Book Trailers: Applications to Use

Group Members

Applications to use to create a book trailer

Application 1. _____

_____

Reasons for choosing this application _____

_____

_____

_____

_____

_____

_____

Application 2. _____

_____

Reasons for choosing this application _____

_____

_____

_____

_____

_____

_____

Application 3. _____

_____

Reasons for choosing this application _____

_____

_____

_____

_____

_____

4. Book Trailers: Brainstorming

Group Members

The Book

Title _____

Characters _____

Genre/Mood _____

What is the book about?

Plot Points _____

_____

_____

Hook _____

_____

_____

Why would someone want to read the book?

Persuade _____

Interest _____

Engage _____

Other details from the book

Exciting _____

Interesting _____

Funny _____

Other _____

5. Book Trailers: Summary

Group Members

You will need to develop a short narration for your book trailer, as well as think about any on-screen captions that you may want to use. You can use the blurb of the book to help you prepare a summary of at least five sentences.

Summary _____

_____
_____
_____
_____
_____
_____
_____
_____
_____
_____
_____
_____
_____
_____
_____

On-screen captions _____

_____
_____
_____
_____
_____
_____
_____

6. Book Trailers: Storyboarding

Group Members

Scene Number _____

Image or Video	**Music** _____
	_____
	_____

On-screen caption _____
_____

Summary sentence _____
_____

Scene Number _____

Image or Video	**Music** _____
	_____
	_____

On-screen caption _____
_____

Summary sentence _____
_____

Scene Number _____

Image or Video	**Music** _____
	_____
	_____

On-screen caption _____
_____

Summary sentence _____
_____

7. Book Trailers: Trailer Finalization Checklist	
Group Members	
Minimum requirements have been met, and at least:	
Production	☐ Five images have been used ☐ One video has been used ☐ One song has been used
Language Use	☐ A five-sentence summary was developed ☐ One sentence is spoken by each group member
Playback	☐ A trailer has been uploaded to YouTube, or it has been saved to a USB drive ☐ The trailer has been tested in the classroom for playback

8. Book Trailers: Pitch it!

Group Members

Use notes and keywords as prompts on your cards for your presentation, so that you can recall the information and keep looking at the audience instead of just reading from a piece of paper. Remember that your aim is to sell your book trailer as being the best. Try to use vocabulary to persuade, engage, and keep your audience interested.

Card 1. _____

_____

Card 2. _____

_____

Card 3. _____

_____

Card 4. _____

_____

Card 5. _____

_____

Card 6. _____

_____

Card 7. _____

_____

Card 8. _____

_____

9. Book Trailers: Book Trailer Evaluation Rubric

Group Members

Plot Hook	A captivating question is used, and the plot is not fully exposed.	1 2 3 4 5
Summary	The summary is concise and does not overwhelm the trailer; on-screen captions are not overused.	1 2 3 4 5
Language	Appropriate vocabulary is applied to help persuade, engage, and keep the audience interested.	1 2 3 4 5
Images	Any images used relate well to the narration, and are representative of the plot.	1 2 3 4 5
Music	The genre of music chosen is reflective of the book.	1 2 3 4 5
Video	Any video used relates well to the narration, is representative of the plot, and works well with the accompanying soundtrack.	1 2 3 4 5
Production	The length is appropriate (under 90 seconds), the voice is not overpowered by music, and the video has a logical progression.	1 2 3 4 5
Copyright	Material used is copyright-free or cited appropriately.	1 2 3 4 5
	TOTAL	**/40**

10. Book Trailers: Critique

Group Members

Write one paragraph identifying at least one good and one bad aspect of the book trailers that your classmates have prepared.

Paragraph 1. _____
_____
_____
_____
_____
_____
_____

Paragraph 2. _____
_____
_____
_____
_____
_____

Paragraph 3. _____
_____
_____
_____
_____
_____

Paragraph 4. _____
_____
_____
_____
_____
_____

11. Book Trailers: WebQuest Evaluation Rubric		
Group Members		
Introduction	Goal of WebQuest achieved.	1 2 3 4 5
Task	All tasks completed, and well executed. ☐ Reviewed five trailers ☐ Created a successful trailer ☐ Presented/pitched a trailer ☐ Evaluated/critiqued others ☐ Voted on the best trailer	1 2 3 4 5 1 2 3 4 5 1 2 3 4 5 1 2 3 4 5 1 2 3 4 5
Process	Students worked well as a team, and the final product is a result of equal collaboration.	1 2 3 4 5
Resources	Ideas expressed are based on all the resources provided, but demonstrated originality.	1 2 3 4 5
Evaluation and Conclusion	Students were able to achieve the final Webquest goals. ☐ Presented as a group, and pitched successfully ☐ One-paragraph critique of others trailers written ☐ Rubric used to identify the best trailer; vote submitted	1 2 3 4 5 1 2 3 4 5 1 2 3 4 5
	TOTAL	**/ 55**

Lesson Plan Guide for VoiceThreading in the Classroom	
Teaching Context	
Level of Proficiency and Maturity	Beginner to advanced. Adaptable for use with young learners through to adults.
Lesson Length	Several lessons (over a week to a term). Homework completion components. Time allotted for each class: 50 minutes.
Lesson Topic	Variable, from portfolio compilation to single topic presentation.
Objectives	1. Enhance communication skills by expressing opinions on a topic, and commenting on others' topics using a variety of methods. 2. Strengthen media literacy and digital literacy skills (use software, images, audio, video, and other media elements or components).
Outcomes	1. Students will create a multimedia-based presentation. 2. Students will employ a range of media resources during their presentation. 3. Students will show evidence of the ability to express personal opinions on a topic, and asynchronously comment on others' topics.
Relevant Prior Learning	Students need to be familiar with using audio recording hardware, and with searching for and compiling multimedia-based resources.

Teacher Preparation	
Hardware	Computer or tablet, with internet access and microphone, camera, and scanner (if scanning resources). USB sticks or Google Drive for storage of resources if needed.
Software	Microsoft Word (if conducting any mind mapping and note-taking). VoiceThread.
Webpage Links	Flickr, Google image search, freemusicarchive.org, VoiceThread.
Additional Resources	VoiceThread creation handout; VoiceThread comment reflection extension activity handout. Both handouts can be used by students in an offline context, and can be completed during class time.

Procedure – Day 1 of 2			
Stage and Timing	**Objective**	**Teacher**	**Students**
Review Stage (10 minutes)	Remind students of the elements that make a good topic presentation. Reintroduce concepts of laying out a topic presentation.	Teacher elicits information from students by asking questions (e.g. what makes a good topic? How do you structure a topic presentation?), with responses to be written on the board.	Students should be able to provide several examples of how to present on a single topic, and provide some example topics.
Warm-up Stage/Pre-Technology Use (15 minutes)	Introduce a VoiceThread by using a teacher-created example.	Show an example VoiceThread with comments as a best practice model.	Students are introduced to a teacher created VoiceThread.

Main Stage (20 minutes)	Develop an initial VoiceThread with students, using the incorporating and constructing a VoiceThread for the Integration in the Classroom handout and resource notes as a guide.	Work through the development of a VoiceThread with students, helping them to develop their first VoiceThread. Introduce new vocabulary as required.	Students work with the teacher, and together, they develop an initial, very basic VoiceThread that contains two or three media artifacts and as many slides with at least one comment.
Lesson Summation Stage/Post-Technology Activities (5 minutes)	Students should be reminded of lesson goals. Individuals can highlight important VoiceThread components, and how to comment.	Remind students of lesson aims. Help them identify key elements of a VoiceThread. Homework: gather resources on a topic idea.	Students should have a good understanding of the workings of a VoiceThread, and be able to make a comment on a slide.

Procedure – Day 2 of 2			
Stage and Timing	Objective	Teacher	Students
Review Stage (10 minutes)	Remind students of their homework, and check that it has been completed.	Teacher ensures that students have collected a variety of resources on a topic (including images, music, and notes).	Students have prepared images to use in a VoiceThread that will present a topic of their choice.
Warm-up Stage/Pre-Technology Use (10 minutes)	The VoiceThread creation handout can be introduced to students.	The teacher works offline with students to help them lay out the structure of their VoiceThread using an associated handout.	Students complete the handout with focus on the aims and goals associated with the development of their VoiceThread and topic.

Main Stage (20 minutes)	Students begin to use the VoiceThread tool to develop and finalize their topic.	The teacher assists students in the development of their VoiceThreads, placing and uploading of media artifacts and in making comments on each slide.	Students successfully sequence their topic presentation using a variety of media artifacts and making a number of comments (at least one per slide).
Lesson Summation Stage/Post-Technology Activities (10 minutes)	Students should have finalized their VoiceThread presentation, or the majority of it, with tidying up and peer commenting set as homework.	Ensure students have successfully completed their VoiceThread, and are ready for peers to comment on it. They should be ready to comment on others.	Students complete their VoiceThread, and share it so that class peers can leave a comment on it for homework.

Further Considerations	
Follow-Up Activities	The VoiceThread comment reflection extension activity handout can be used in a follow-up lesson to help prompt students' thinking regarding the comments left on their VoiceThread by their peers. It can also serve as a means to evaluate how the use of VoiceThread has gone over with your students, and what areas could be improved with a future implementation.
Contingency Plan(s)	The use of the handout used in Warm-Up Stage/Pre-Technology use on Day 2 can be extended, and used to fill a full class hour. However, if this is not used at this time, then the next lesson in the course syllabus should be ready in case there is a problem with using the VoiceThread website or any other technology.
Evaluation	What are the biggest frustrations for implementation? Can these be remedied next time? What are the successes of the lesson? What did students get out of this activity? Can more language practice be provided?

Example Implementation:
VoiceThread

The Teaching and Learning Context

VoiceThreads are an effective way for all students, at any language level, to begin practicing speaking. VoiceThread development also allows for the practice of a variety of computer-based skills alongside language practice, and offer students the ability to listen and go over content as many times as they wish before having to share it with their peers, the teacher, or other stakeholders. For students then, it can serve as a tool that allows them to share their ideas, listen to others and respond by talking; for teachers it can serve as a means of providing assessment that can be easily moderated and graded, as all work is distributed in a central location. Essentially, VoiceThreads can provide every student with a voice, and every student the ability to comment, after being able to think through what it is that they want to say and present.

Teaching Material

The teaching material can be broken down into three: the software, the hardware, and the tasks and activities behind the learning content.

The software

The software is the VoiceThread application, depending on device used, or the VoiceThread website accessible through any browser. The software is intuitive enough for a broad range of learners to be able to become familiar with it in a short time frame, and be able to embed content, comment, and share easily.

The hardware

The hardware is a device capable of accessing the VoiceThread website or using the VoiceThread application, and has a built-in microphone (for voice comments) or web camera (for video comments). The device should have the ability to work with the documents that can be imported into a VoiceThread as well, including image files (such as, JPG), Microsoft PowerPoint and Word files, PDF files, and video files (like MP4).

Learning content

Due to the flexibility behind the types of documents that a VoiceThread can house, and the means of providing comments on them, the learning content will vary on an activity-to-activity basis. It will, however, reflect the content that students are working on during class or for homework.

Procedure

As with a lot of technology use in the classroom, it may prove best to use one item per term or semester, so that students can become familiar with it and complete all their assignments or tasks when using it. This could prove especially the case with a site like VoiceThread, where students can comment using a variety of modes (by recording audio or video, or by typing or annotating), and use it to showcase a variety of media. To this end, a number of potential activities are introduced to illustrate the range of ideas that can be applied to the use of VoiceThread in the TESOL setting. The ideas presented here are provided as examples, and are meant to illustrate how a VoiceThread can be adapted and applied to learning. Ultimately, you will need to decide how best to adapt and implement activities from your classes to the world of VoiceThread. The challenge will be to ensure that all students are able to record their voice or response so that it is clear and audible to all.

Week one – TeacherThreads

To start students out with VoiceThreading, it is a good idea to create a sample thread which can be used to show students how to embed content, and the various means of how to comment on that content. In this way, the first VoiceThread is used as a tutorial and for practice where students become familiar with how to view, use, and comment on the site and the application. It serves as an icebreaker to the tool.

Week two – StudentThreads

The second VoiceThread should be a short VoiceThread created by the students themselves. If each student works solo, then you can discover where problems for each individual might reside, be they technical or linguistic. Alternatively, students working in groups can help each other solve any technical problems or any other issues that might arise, but this may see the more challenged students not able to produce their own VoiceThreads at a later date.

Week three – ActivityThreads

VoiceThreads can then focus on aspects of content including vocabulary, pronunciation, and writing. Assignments should now become ones where students create their own VoiceThreads, working by themselves or with peers, upload them, share them with the class, and begin to comment on the material. Of course, teacher-initiated VoiceThreads and prompts can also be used to target specific areas or use of required content in a variety of different ways. Several example activities are included here.

BookThread

Students can use VoiceThread as a presentation medium to provide a book review, with other students giving their opinion on the book in the comments. Students can upload an image of the book, or they can develop a book trailer as part of their presentation. This could follow on from a digital storytelling project or from a WebQuest on book trailers.

DirectionsThread

Students can provide a map of their route to school, or how to get to one of their favorite places from school. This could link to a unit on directions.

EssayThread

Students can either upload their entire essay as a file for others to read and then comment on. For shorter essays, students can provide the text and read it aloud, and other students can then provide spoken or written feedback on the work.

PreviewThread

Each week, a VoiceThread could be used to introduce the class topic, with specific questions set to have students think about the topic, or to answer using set phrases or expressions. This may lead to more students willing to respond in class, as they have already practiced using the content at home, and uploaded this to the VoiceThread before coming to class.

StoryThread

Students develop a story by responding to peer photographs with a voice comment. Each student takes a photo of something that they find interesting while on their way to school. This can be uploaded to a VoiceThread with the next student commenting on the photograph, before uploading one of his or her own, which the next student will comment upon. The teacher can provide a photograph for the first student to respond to, and the teacher can respond to the last student's photograph in order to close the story.

TestPracticeThread

A number of test practice contents can be adapted for use as part of a VoiceThread, from the International English Language Testing System (IELTS) to the Test of English for International Communication (TOEIC). For example, in TOEIC, students need to be able to predict questions regarding a photo or be able to describe a photo. In VoiceThread, students can be presented with a photograph, and they can leave a comment to describe it. This also gives students the chance to practice their pronunciation, intonation, grammar, vocabulary, and the cohesiveness of their description, all of which are points examined during the speaking component of the TOEIC.

TextBookThread

Any page from a textbook can be uploaded into a VoiceThread for students to comment on, and this can include providing a picture and inviting brainstorming on a topic, uploading text that students need to provide an opinion on, and delivering a cloze exercise where each student has to speak the completed sentence as a comment (with enough sentences for students to record one comment each).

TongueTwisterThread

Each student can be asked to make a voice comment while having to read a series of tongue twisters. This provides teachers with a means of quickly assessing the pronunciation skills of all students, and provides them with the means to practice pronunciation and to hear their peers' pronunciation.

Example tongue twisters include:
- Lovely Lucy loves lucky Larry.
- She sells seashells by the seashore.
- How much wood would a woodchuck chuck if a woodchuck could chuck wood?

- Red rabbits rush to the right really rudely.
- Red leather, yellow leather.
- Peter Piper picked a pack of pickled peppers.
- Thirty-three thieves rushed through the thick thorny thicket last Thursday.

TutorialThread

Students can illustrate how they use various tools, like Daum Maps (map.daum.net) or Google Maps (maps.google.com), to get to specific places, and this can match to a lesson on directions or to a lesson on travel. These kinds of VoiceThreads can also demonstrate how to perform specific tasks with students uploading demonstration videos. Students could show others how to prepare and cook their favorite dish while providing the recipe, and this can link to a lesson on food or shopping. If the setting allows, the food could then be brought to a final class party.

VideoResponseThread

The teacher can post a video to a VoiceThread, such as a short TedTalk or a silent short film, and students can respond to it. If a TEDTalk is used, students can either respond to specific questions or comment about something interesting or new that they have learned while watching the video. If a silent short film is used, then students can comment on the sequence of events, if the task is to practice this kind of language.

Lesson Plan Guide for Blogging	
Teaching Context	
Level of Proficiency and Maturity	Beginner to advanced. Adaptable for use with young learners through to adults.
Lesson Length	Suitable for a couple of lessons over a week. Homework completion components. Time allotted for each class: 50 minutes.
Lesson Topic	Food, cooking.
Objectives	1. Enhance communication skills through collaborative learning, presentations, and writing and speaking development. 2. Strengthen multiple literacies (computer literacy, digital literacy, and English literacy).
Outcomes	1. Students identify significant points on a topic, and use these in to develop blog posts and presentations. 2. Transfer current knowledge into learning, using and understanding technological systems.
Relevant Prior Learning	None required. Blogging and wiki experiences helpful.

Teacher Preparation	
Hardware	Computers or tablets with internet access for each group of students. USB sticks or Google Drive for storage.
Software	WordPress applications, or access to the website. Access to various media for development support (e.g. Google Images, and YouTube).
Webpage Links	WordPress.com www.epicurious.com www.taste.com.au Other food and cooking websites as appropriate to student level and age group.
Additional Resources	Handouts*: • Pre-blog teacher considerations • Pre-blog student considerations • How to write a blog post • Peer checklist – Blog post

*Available under 'Photocopiable material'.

Procedure – Day 1 of 3			
Stage and Timing	**Objective**	**Teacher**	**Students**
Introductory Stage (5 minutes)	The topic of food and cooking is introduced. Traditional dishes for the host country can be provided to students.	Introduce the traditional foods of their country, and their favorite traditional dishes.	Students begin to think about their country and the traditional dishes that are their favorites.
Warm-up Stage/Pre-Technology Use (20 minutes)	Students work in small groups, to discuss each other's traditional foods and favorite traditional dishes.	Assist students as required. Provide question prompts: What are your country's traditional foods? What is your favorite traditional food? How is it prepared?	Students work together to discusses each other's traditional foods, their favorite traditional dishes, and how these are prepared.

Main Stage (15 minutes)	Students present their traditional foods to the class, and their favorite food.	The presentation can be used as an assessment if desired.	Students should each provide a short one-minute presentation.
Lesson Summation Stage/Post-Technology Activities (5 minutes)	Homework is set for students to either video themselves preparing the food, or finding a video of someone else preparing their food. The audio must be in English, or the student can provide an English voice-over.	Provide links to various cooking websites that may prove useful (e.g. Epicurious, Taste).	Students will prepare a video of themselves preparing their favorite traditional food, or a link to someone else preparing it.

Procedure – Day 2 of 3			
Stage and Timing	**Objective**	**Teacher**	**Students**
Review Stage (5 minutes)	Go over the class content from the previous lesson, and provide a short introduction on how to edit with a blog.	Confirm that the students have created a video, or have found a link to one suitable to use with blogging.	Students should have prepared a video, or have a link to one that is suitable.
Warm-up Stage/Pre-Technology Use (5 minutes)	Provide student access to the teacher-prepared blog page, and tips on editing with it (e.g. how to add a link, add an image, upload a file or embed a video).	Ensure that all students can access the blog, and are able to work with the editor. Review the 'Pre-blog teacher' handout*.	Students should be able to log onto the blog site, and begin working with the post editor. Have students review the 'Pre-blog student' handout*.

*Available under 'Photocopiable material'.

Main Stage (35 minutes)	Students work in groups of three to assist each other in creating a recipe page on the blog for their dishes.	Provide student groups with a layout to follow (e.g. picture of dish, recipe: ingredients and procedure, then a video of food preparation and cooking.	Students work in groups to assist each other in developing their posts, working with the 'How to write a blog post' handout*, as well as the guidelines for the post-format.
Lesson Summation Stage/Post-Technology Activities (5 minutes)	Students should have their post at a ready-to-publish stage, and need to review it a final time.	Ensure that all students have completed their blog page successfully. Provide the 'Peer checklist – Blog post' handout* for homework.	All components of the blog post should be complete, and the post published. Students will review another blog for homework using the handout provided.

*Available under 'Photocopiable material'.

Procedure – Day 3 of 3			
Stage and Timing	**Objective**	**Teacher**	**Students**
Review Stage (5 minutes)	Students are reminded of their homework, and that they should submit their completed checklists to their peers.	Ensure that all of the peer checklists are distributed to students for review.	Students review the checklist, and if necessary ask questions to their peers about it.
Warm-up Stage/Pre-Technology Use (15 minutes)	Blog post review.	Ensure that students have access to their blog, and are able to edit their posts if they wish.	Students edit their post while taking into consideration the feedback provided by their peers.

Main Stage (20 minutes)	Individual presentations answering: What is the dish? Why is it a favorite? How is it made? What does it taste like?	Students will give a short presentation of their blog post (perhaps one to two minutes each)*.	Students provide a presentation regarding their dish, and how to prepare it.
Lesson Summation Stage/Post-Technology Activities (10 minutes)	Share the blog content with various stakeholders as appropriate. Lock the blog posts from any further edits, comments, and replies.	Assist students in sharing their blog post with peers or parents.	Students can archive their post in an offline portfolio, or share it with others.

*An extra day will be required for presentations if the class is a large one.

Further Considerations	
Follow-Up Activities	If the teaching context allows, students can demonstrate in the classroom. Excursion to a local market. Activities relating to festivals and culture.
Contingency Plan(s)	The next lesson in the course syllabus should be ready in case there is a problem at any stage of blog development. Alternatively, some language games can be prepared to fill in the time if technological problems occur. Several activity sheets for review of previous material should be prepared to allow those students who complete their scripts or recording to keep busy with language content.
Evaluation	What are the biggest frustrations for implementation? Can these be remedied next time? What are the successes of the lesson? What did students get out of this activity? Can more language practice be provided?

Example Implementation:
Blogs

The Teaching and Learning Context

A wide range of possibilities exist for the use of blogs with second-language learners. A blog can be used for a single class period to develop, revise, and then post a paragraph or an entire article, and blogs can be applied over a semester or term when working on more extensive projects or a series of pieces for a portfolio. For the latter case, the example of implementation presented in this section of the book presents a ten week outline for the development of a variety of language skills over the course of a term. It is suitable for developing blog use with students who are studying in a general English communication program within a college or university setting. The tasks and activities can be adapted to suit a variety of approaches that include communicative language teaching (CLT), task-based language learning (TBL), competency based language learning (CBLL), or project-based language learning (PBLL). The project selected here is that of developing an online newspaper called The Global Times.

Teaching Material

When using blogs in the classroom, the teaching material can be broken down into three parts: the software, the hardware, and the activities or tasks selected as appropriate for the learning context.

The software

Depending on your teaching context, the choice of blog software varies. It generally comes down to a matter of how accessible the content can be. For example closed for use with very young learners providing them with a safe-harbor environment from which to work; open at a global level for anyone to view and comment on when used with adults. The resources list presents several choices and there should be at least one that potentially offers the best options for your intended use and with which you feel comfortable when using with your students. It is likely that this choice will also come down to the ages of your students as well as the teaching locale (for example, grade school, university, or private institute).

The hardware

Depending on how and where the blog is to be accessed by students, a number of different technological requirements regarding hardware will need to be met. If you are working in a bring-your-own-device (BYOD) environment, you will need to make sure that the students bring their devices as required, and that they have the associated applications installed. If students are using the computers available at school, then the computer lab or computer room may need to be booked. If you are setting blog use for homework, then you will need to ensure that students are all students are able to access the hardware required to complete any set blog work and to use the internet. An alternate is to have students work on blog posts during class time in a traditional manner, using pen and paper, and then digitizing this for homework.

Learning content

A wide variety of tasks and activities are suited to blog use, with the tasks and activities chosen depending on the age and maturity levels of learners, their language level, the teaching environment (grade school, university, private institute), and the desired learning outcomes.

Procedure

For blog use to be successful, it is important to keep posts updated. It is also important to set clear expectations for learning goals with a means to engage students in the learning process as they work on their blogs, and to ensure that they are working collaboratively to meet these goals. What they are in turn developing can be adequately assessed for improvement in their learning and language abilities, and is able to be showcased. For this to occur, blog use will require active participation on the part of students, and this participation can be conducted in an asynchronous manner, providing them with time to compose comments or replies, as well edit blog posts. The editorial control on offer through the medium can also grant students a sense of ownership and responsibility to the site and the contents that they develop. To this end, and to maintain interest in blog projects, it may also be prudent to incorporate aspects of students' posts, comments, and replies within classroom discussions. Yet, no matter how blogs are used in the classroom, it is important to evaluate and take into account aspects of how students are using the avenue for communication, and producing the content that results.

Week one – Blog familiarization

When starting out using a blog, it is advisable to provide an introduction to the software that has been chosen, and familiarize students with the mechanics of how to post and edit blog articles, comment, moderate comments, and reply. This can be achieved by using a screencast, along with an associated worksheet, so that students are able to engage in language practice while becoming familiar with the blog process and what will be required of them throughout the remainder of the course. An overview of the tasks and objectives intended to be achieved by the end of blog use will also be important to introduce to students here, so that they can understand why they need to be familiar with blog use, how it all ties in to their learning goals, and how it can benefit their language skills.

Week two – Newspaper project

Students are informed of the topics, how the online newspaper project will be conducted, and that each group will ultimately be responsible for developing content for one of six sections of The Global Times newspaper. These sections can align strictly with textbook topics, or they could be developed to align with student interests, hobbies, or associations of which they are members. Each group of students can work on the same section each week, with the best aspects of each group's content making the final contribution to an official newspaper article on that topic.

Week three – Advice columns

This week can see students prepare questions that they would like to have advice on, with another group then researching and preparing answers. Alternatively, the teacher can provide the questions with appropriate links to obtain the answers. This kind of activity would be able to dovetail with a number of units, including those on injuries and seeing a doctor through to those providing guidance on study skills.

Week four – Reviews one

For this week, students could develop a digital story, with associated images and video components to review a book, movie, or an event like a concert. This could be completed in conjunction with a unit on entertainment, or hobbies.

Week five – Reviews two

Following on from the previous review, students could review a meal at a local restaurant using a rating scale that they have developed. Students would be able to review any restaurant on or near their campus, with appropriate images, and this can be completed in conjunction with a unit on food or cooking.

Week six – Recipe

Students can develop a written recipe based on their favorite food. The recipe would need to detail the ingredients, preparation, and method accurately, and include a photo of the prepared dish as well as an accompanying step-by-step video. This can tie to a unit on food or cooking.

Week seven – Tours

Students can develop a virtual tour using their smartphone to make video and audio recordings and to take photos. They could develop a walking tour of the campus. Alternatively, they could create a neighborhood tour, highlighting the best places to do certain activities in that area of town. This could dovetail with a unit on family and home life, school, or directions.

Week eight – Interviews

An example task for this week could see students conducting interviews on campus with native English speaking teachers. They would need to be able to develop appropriate interview questions on their topic, as well as have the necessary hardware to video or audio record their interview. The interview media could then be posted to the blog with an associated written summary underneath.

Week nine – Finalization

In this week of blog use, students would need to polish their articles by conducting last minute edits, taking peer comments into consideration, and selecting the final best pieces from all groups' articles to complete their section of the newspaper.

Week ten – Launch party

In this week of the class, students would be able to present one section of the blog as part of an 'official' newspaper launch.

This can be completed as a class activity with another class, or with other stakeholders invited to attend.

Lesson Plan Guide for Wikis	
Teaching Context	
Level of Proficiency and Maturity	Beginner to advanced. Adaptable for use with young learners through to adults.
Lesson Length	Suitable for several lessons over a week. Homework completion components. Time allotted for each class: 50 minutes.
Lesson Topic	Travel
Objectives	1. Enhance communication skills through collaborative learning, presentations, and writing and speaking development. 2. Strengthen multiple literacies (computer literacy, digital literacy, and English literacy).
Outcomes	1. Students identify significant points on a topic, and use these in a presentation based on wiki articles that they have developed. 2. Transfer current knowledge into learning, using and understanding technological systems.
Relevant Prior Learning	None required. Blogging and wiki experiences helpful.

Teacher Preparation	
Hardware	Computers or tablets with internet access for each group of students working together. USB sticks or Google Drive for storage.
Software	Online wiki software (e.g. PBWorks). Access to various media for development support (e.g. Google Images, and YouTube).
Webpage Links	PBworks.com www.lonelyplanet.com www.tripadvisor.com (other travel sites appropriate to student language level and age group)
Additional Resources	Handouts*: Pre-wiki teacher considerations Pre-wiki student considerations How to write a wiki article Peer checklist – Wiki article

*Available under 'Photocopiable material'.

Procedure – Day 1 of 3			
Stage and Timing	Objective	Teacher	Students
Introductory Stage (15 minutes)	Students bring a souvenir item from a trip to class, and use it to introduce the topic of travel.	Students need to be reminded to bring their item at least a week before, as well as the day prior.	Students will talk about their item in front of the class for at least one minute.
Warm-up Stage/Pre-Technology Use (5 minutes)	Students work in groups to create a travel wiki on a specific country, with page topics on: a short history of the nation, 'must see' sites, best times to travel, daily budget, and foods to eat.	Divide the class into groups, and provide them with suggestions to start creating their wiki articles and pages on a specific country.	Students form groups, and decide on the country that they will be creating wiki articles about, and who will be the main person responsible for each topic.

Main Stage (20 minutes)	Brainstorming and resource collection. Using websites and collecting various media. The final product should contain at least 50 words a topic for beginners, 100 words for intermediate students, and 200 words for advanced students.	Teacher assists students in brainstorming ideas on each topic, and for each article that the students will write. Teachers can take this opportunity to go through the 'pre-wiki teacher considerations' handout*.	Students begin to form points for their article and collect associated images (e.g. pictures and video).
Lesson Summation Stage/Post-Technology Activities (10 minutes)	Students are assigned additional wiki roles, and are provided with the 'pre-wiki student considerations' handout*.	Introduce students to the additional roles that they need to play when working on their wiki.	Students select who becomes the article editor, the citation editor, and the chief editor.

*Available under 'Photocopiable material'.

Procedure – Day 2 of 3			
Stage and Timing	**Objective**	**Teacher**	**Students**
Review Stage (5 minutes)	Go over the class content from the previous lesson, and provide a short introduction on how to edit with a wiki.	Confirm that students have prepared notes and various media that relates to their assigned topic, and are ready to create their wiki page.	Students should have prepared notes and media ready to create a wiki article on their topic.
Warm-up Stage/Pre-Technology Use (5 minutes)	Students post their articles under the main travel section page of the teacher-developed wiki.	The teacher helps students to post their pages to the designated areas of the wiki.	Students prepare to edit their wiki article, and enrich it with media.

Main Stage (30 minutes)	Students complete their wiki article on the topics they have chosen using the handout provided.	Help students work through the handout to develop their wiki article.	Students work through the 'how to write a wiki-article' handout* to develop their wiki page.
Lesson Summation Stage/Post-Technology Activities (5 minutes)	Provide students with the 'peer checklist – wiki article' handout*, so that they can complete it for their fellow members' articles. Inform students that they will need to present the information about their country in the next class session.	Ensure that students will be able to complete their articles for homework, if not already complete, and that they need to take into consideration the suggestions from the 'peer checklist – wiki article'*.	Students will complete, and then pass the 'peer checklist – wiki article'* to peers. All students will complete their article by the end of class, or they will need to do so for homework.

*Available under 'photocopiable material'.

Procedure – Day 3 of 3			
Stage and Timing	**Objective**	**Teacher**	**Students**
Review Stage (5 minutes)	Go over the previous class content, and remind students that their wiki articles and in-class presentations are due.	Confirm that students have completed their wiki articles, and are ready to practice their presentation.	Wiki articles should be fully developed, with the students ready to present them.
Warm-up Stage/Pre-Technology Use (10 minutes)	Provide time for students to practice going through their presentation.	Ensure that all students are ready to present and provide guidance for those students who still require it.	Students practice delivering their presentations together.

Main Stage (20 minutes)	Presentations delivered, and assessment completed.	Assess student presentations and wiki work using prefabricated rubrics, such as those provided in the evaluation section.	Students present their wiki travel articles to the class for assessment.
Lesson Summation Stage/Post-Technology Activities (10 minutes)	Archive wiki content, and share the material with various stakeholders as appropriate. Lock the wiki pages from further edits.	Assist students in archiving their wiki pages, or in sharing the content with their peers or parents.	Students can archive their wiki pages offline, or share them with others.

Further Considerations	
Follow-Up Activities	A follow-up activity might include planning itineraries for a trip to each of the countries students gave their presentations on. Students could be assigned to create a dialog based on that of a travel agent and a client wanting to book a holiday.
Contingency Plan(s)	The next lesson in the course syllabus should be ready in case there is a problem at any stage of wiki development. Alternatively, some language games can be prepared to fill in the time if technological problems occur. Several activity sheets for review of previous material should be prepared to allow those students who complete their scripts or recording to keep busy with language content.
Evaluation	What are the biggest frustrations for implementation? Can these be remedied next time? What are the successes of the lesson? What did students get out of this activity? Can more language practice be provided?

Example Implementation:
Wikis

The Teaching and Learning Context

A wiki can be used for a single class period to review and edit a single paragraph or an entire academic article. Wikis could be applied over a semester or term when working on a more extensive projects or a series of portfolio pieces. The following procedural example presents a ten week outline for the development of article writing and presentation skills, and can be applied with adults over the course of a term in an English for academic purposes (EAP) class in a private institute, college, or university setting.

Teaching Material

When using wikis in the classroom, the teaching material can be broken down into three: the software, the hardware, and the activities or tasks selected as appropriate for the learning context.

The software

Depending on your teaching context, the choice of wiki software will vary. Generally, this comes down to one of two choices either installing wiki software locally and hosting your own wiki, or using existing wiki software that is hosted by a company on the internet. The resources list presents several choices and there should be at least one that potentially offers the best options for your intended use and with which you feel comfortable using with your students. It is likely that this choice will also come down to the ages of your students as well as the teaching locale (for example, grade school, university, or private institute).

The hardware

Depending on how and where the wiki will be accessed by students, a number of different technological requirements regarding hardware will need to be met. If you are working in a bring-your-own-device (BYOD) context, you will need to make sure that the students bring their devices as required and that they have the associated applications installed. If students are using the computers available at school, then the computer lab or computer room may need to be booked. If you are setting wiki use for homework, then you will need to ensure that all students are able to access the hardware required to complete any set wiki work and to use the internet.

The Learning content

A wide variety of tasks and activities are suited to wiki use, and the tasks chosen should take into account the age and maturity levels of learners, their language level, the teaching environment (grade school, university, private institute), and the desired learning outcomes.

Procedure

Wiki use is adaptable to almost any class and learning environment, but their use must be pedagogically sound. The reason for this is that wiki use will see students work together to create knowledge, and develop learning material that is tailored to their learning context. In this regard, individual authorship becomes less important than working collaboratively to successfully complete the outcomes set for the task or project being developed. It is therefore important to regulate and structure the interaction that students have with wikis so that any content produced, edited, and created is completed with these objectives in mind.

Foord (A6 Training, 2016) has developed the STOLEN acronym to identify aspects of wiki use that can increase the potential of wikis working well in the classroom context, and for teachers to use as a guide when starting out. This acronym is a useful one to keep in mind when using wikis in any teaching and learning context, and it can be broken down as follows:

- **S**pecific overall objective – set objectives that are clear and understood by all, and this can be guided by providing example pages and templates.
- **T**imely – set time limits and create a wiki with a specific purpose, and with a specific end point to assignments.
- **O**wnership – create ownership in the collaborative wiki space, as this will allow for students to be creative and to make their pages their own.
- **L**ocalized objective – establish assignments that allow for familiarization with the wiki at the start as well as the type of use that you envision for it before moving on to more complicated, longer, or bigger tasks.
- **E**ngagement rules – determine who can edit the wiki and to what degree, and develop acceptable and unacceptable guidelines for use.
- **N**avigation – establish a simple and clear navigational structure this will ensure that wiki content can be easily found and that the structure is easily duplicated by students.

Keep in mind that it is not in and of itself the use of technology that provides learning, but the pedagogy behind it that leads to learning. Careful consideration therefore needs to go into the tasks and activities that students will perform when using a wiki, and how these tasks and activities come to relate to the specific learning outcomes of the course.

Week one – Wiki familiarization

When using a wiki over the course of a term or semester, it is advisable to provide an introduction to the wiki software that will be used, along with some familiarization of what kind of mechanical tasks that students will be expected to perform when using the wiki. This can be achieved by presenting students with a screencast and an associated worksheet so that they can also engage in language learning while becoming familiar with the wiki, and exactly what it is that they will need to be doing with the application throughout the remainder of the course. An overview of the tasks and objectives intended to be achieved by the end of wiki use will also be important to present to students here, so that they can understand why they need to be familiar with wiki use, how it all ties in to their learning goals, and how it can benefit both their language learning and academic skills.

Week two – Editing

Students will need to become familiar with how to edit articles in a wiki environment, and this means being able to understand and use wiki markup language. Again a screencast could be useful here, but perhaps a demonstration and students practicing in the wiki sandbox may be more beneficial. Depending on the objectives of the assignment, you may also want to introduce other factors at this stage to relate the editing process back to the learning objectives and overall outcomes. This could mean going over what constitutes a good article, and how to structure and compose a successful wiki article.

Week three – Exploring the topic

Depending on the topic set for assignment, this week of the course will vary. If you are going to have students explore a topic based on themes that can be expanded into a written article for submission, then one means of exploring the topic might be looking at Wikipedia stubs, and seeing how these topics can be expanded to form a fully developed article. This can also lead into teaching aspects of mind mapping, and how to develop topic outlines when writing. Students can work collaboratively to brainstorm on the topic, and put their ideas in point form or graphic form on the wiki.

Week four – Applying sources

This week of the course could be spent familiarizing students with school policies regarding aspects of copyright and plagiarism. This is important as sometimes determining what is and is not plagiarism can be very difficult for students who are just starting to write more academic style essays. Also being able to write citations correctly in the necessary style of their field of study can also prove to be a challenge. The American Psychological Association (APA), Modern Language Association (MLA), or Harvard referencing styles can then be introduced as a necessary part of academic life.

Week five – Selecting articles

Students need to select a topic, or be provided with a series of choices from the teacher, and begin to find sources that they can reference when constructing their own article. If students are new to the academic setting, this may also prove to be a challenge for them. It may be necessary to teach how to read an abstract, how to identify keywords, how to scan articles, and how to take notes. Sources that students have identified as being useful can then be used as a start in building their bibliography list on the wiki. So too, any sources collated could be used to develop an annotated bibliography with students working on this process either individually or collaboratively.

Week six – Drafting articles

In this week, students begin to write their articles, either editing 'live' or from the sandbox. Students can work collaboratively or individually on developing a summary of what they intend to discuss in their article, fleshing out their previously constructed outlines. The remainder of the writing task can be set as a homework activity, or continued on in the following class sessions.

Week seven – Providing and receiving feedback

After completing a first draft, it is important to get feedback and have fellow students edit other students' articles. It is a good idea to use a checklist for this purpose that can highlight the positives and negatives of the article itself as well as wiki use. Just such a checklist is included in the photocopiable section of this book. Students can also be assigned to look over peer work for grammatical and spelling errors, and to offer suggestions for vocabulary changes and style changes (for example, high modality to low modality).

Week eight – Feedback responses

This week can be used to review the feedback provided by students on others' work, and common problems, mistakes, and errors can be worked through together. This point of the course can also serve as a reminder for students as to what they have achieved and learned so far, and how the wiki is leading to the development of their academic and language skills.

Week nine – Presentations

At this point, all articles have been edited and peer reviewed. They can now be summarized and, along with appropriate media elements, be provided to the class through oral presentations. This can be done individually or collaboratively, with students presenting either their own article or that of other class members. This provides them with the practice in summarizing academic articles that is expected in any academic seminar, and presenting the content in their own words along with an interpretation of their own understanding of the content.

Week ten – Assignment submission

Each stage of article development and culmination in a summary presentation can be graded either as a whole or in part. An appropriate grading scheme would need to be developed, and this would need to cover the outline, the bibliography (annotated or not), the article, and the presentation.

6. Photocopiable Material

6. Photocopiable Material

This section contains photocopiable content, and you are free to make as many copies as you require for teaching purposes and preparing your classes. Any other use or distribution should include a citation to the source of the content. In developing your WebQuests, VoiceThreads, blogs and wikis, it will prove useful to use the provided resource notes and handouts as a guide.

The lesson plan template can be used for considering how best to integrate the steps for using WebQuests, VoiceThreads, blogs and wikis with your classes. As such, the template is meant to act as a means to think about how to implement, with your classes, aspects of what has been discovered through this book. The template should be supplemented with any necessary material, along with the staging as well as other aspects of the lesson being adjusted as required.

The following photocopiable material is available:

General
- Lesson plan template

WebQuests
- WebQuest worksheet resource notes
- WebQuest worksheet

VoiceThread
- Incorporating and constructing a VoiceThread for integration into the classroom resource notes
- VoiceThread creation resource notes
- VoiceThread creation handout
- VoiceThread comment reflection extension activity resource notes
- VoiceThread comment reflection extension activity handout

Blogs and wikis
- Pre-blog/pre-wiki teacher considerations
- Pre-blog/pre-wiki student considerations
- How to write a blog post resource notes
- How to write a blog post handout
- Peer checklist – Blog post
- How to write a wiki article resource notes
- How to write a wiki article handout
- Peer checklist – Wiki article

Lesson Plan Template	
Teaching Context	
Level of Proficiency and Maturity	
Lesson Length	
Lesson Topic	
Objective	
Outcomes	
Relevant Prior Learning	
Teacher Preparation	
Hardware	
Software	
Webpage Links	
Additional Resources	

Procedure			
Stage and Timing	Objective	Teacher	Students
Review Stage (if required)			
Warm-up Stage/Pre-Technology Use			
Main Stage/ Technology-based Activity			
Practice Stage			
Lesson Summation Stage/Post-Technology Activities			

Further Considerations	
Follow-Up Activities	
Contingency Plan(s)	
Evaluation	

WebQuest Worksheet Resource Notes	
Title	Choose a title for the WebQuest, and write it here.
Introduction/Description	Provide an overview and set up any role-playing scenario (e.g. 'You are a linguist investigating the pronunciation of Standard American English').
Task	Describe the end product of activities here. Include details of questions to be answered; details to be analysed, summarized, or organized; positions adopted or to be defended; and so on.
Process	List a step-by-step process for students to follow when completing the task(s).
Resources	Include all required resources and website links, annotated with a brief description.
Evaluation	Develop or utilise a prefabricated rubric to assess students.
Conclusion	Summarize what learners need to accomplish by the end of the WebQuest. Include questions to assist in transferring the knowledge gained to a broader context.

WebQuest Worksheet	
Title	
Introduction/Description	
Task	
Process	
Resources	
Evaluation	
Conclusion	

Incorporating and Constructing a VoiceThread for Integration into the Classroom Resource Notes
VoiceThread goal
State the learning outcome or the intended direction of the VoiceThread below.
Intended direction
Explicitly express the educational focus or aim behind the VoiceThread here.
Learning outcome(s): State the primary learning objective here. State the secondary, or any other, learning objective(s) here.
Potential media artifacts
List artifacts by type, and describe the rationale behind how each meets the intended direction of the VoiceThread and any desired learning outcome(s).
Documents
List all the artifacts required to create the VoiceThread.
Document rationale: List how each artifact meets the VoiceThread direction or learning outcome(s)
Images
List all the images necessary for the VoiceThread.
Image rationale: List how each image meets the VoiceThread direction or a learning outcome(s).
Video
List all the video required for the VoiceThread.
Video rationale: List how each video meets the VoiceThread direction or learning outcome(s).

Model comments

Write out some ideas for initial comments per slide, expand as necessary, and determine the best format.

Slide 1 comment type

Voice, typed, uploaded audio, webcam, narration.

Comment: Draft comments here.

Slide 2 comment type

Voice, typed, uploaded audio, webcam, narration.

Comment: Draft comments here.

Slide 3 comment Type

Voice, typed, uploaded audio, webcam, narration.

Comment: Draft comments here.

Notes

Make any additional notes here.

VoiceThread Creation Resource Notes

VoiceThread Title	Group Members
A title is chosen by students, and written here.	Student names are listed here.

Slide Number
Write the slide number being worked on here.

Media Resources (choice of media and why)	Focus (aim/goal/learning outcome)	Comment (format and wording)
Sketch an example to reflect what will appear on this slide of your VoiceThread. Keep in mind that the document, image, or video that you select must match the comments that you will make regarding it, and align with the focus or goal that you are trying to communicate.	What are you trying to communicate or achieve with your VoiceThread – is there an intended learning outcome? What is the aim or goal of your VoiceThread?	What format will your comment take? (Consider voice-only, webcam, use of the notation tool). What comment will you leave on this slide? (Write out your comment here).

VoiceThread Creation Handout		
VoiceThread Title		**Group Members**
Slide Number		
Media Resources (choice of media and why)	**Focus (aim/goal/learning outcome)**	**Comment (format and wording)**
Slide Number		
Media Resources (choice of media and why)	**Focus (aim/goal/learning outcome)**	**Comment (format and wording)**

VoiceThread Comment Reflection Extension Activity Resource Notes		
VoiceThread Title		**Student Names**
A title is chosen by students, and written here.		Student names are listed here.
Reflection Questions	**Example**	**Reason**
What comment(s) did you find particularly interesting?	Write the comment(s) here.	State what made the comment(s) interesting.
What comment(s) did you particularly agree with?	Write the comment(s) here.	State why you agree with the comment(s).
What comment(s) did you particularly disagree with?	Write the comment(s) here.	State why you disagree with the comment(s).
What comment(s) made you change the way that you think?	Write the comment(s) here.	State how your thinking changed.
What was the most challenging aspect of VoiceThread for you?	Write the aspect(s) here.	State your reason(s) here.
What new vocabulary or expression(s) did you learn?	Write the new term(s) here.	Write the meaning(s) here.
What other thing(s) did you learn when using VoiceThread?	Write the other thing(s) learned here.	How did you learn about the thing(s) listed?

VoiceThread Comment Reflection Extension Activity		
VoiceThread Title		**Student Names**
Reflection Questions	**Example**	**Reason**
What comment(s) did you find particularly interesting?		
What comment(s) did you particularly agree with?		
What comment(s) did you particularly disagree with?		
What comment(s) made you change the way that you think?		
What was the most challenging aspect of VoiceThread for you?		
What new vocabulary or expressions did you learn?		
What other thing(s) did you learn when using VoiceThread?		

Pre-Blog/Pre-Wiki Teacher Considerations
Consider the following elements when utilizing blogs and wikis in the classroom.

Procedural Elements
1. School policies for blog/wiki use have been consulted
2. Parental consent has been obtained where required
3. Students are all aware of safe internet practices

Technical Elements
1. An appropriate blog/wiki tool has been selected
2. Familiarity with site settings for the selected blog/wiki
3. Familiarity with how to post/edit with the selected blog/wiki
4. Settings adjusted on the blog/wiki as appropriate
5. An aggregator has been selected for use

Pedagogical Elements
1. Length of blog/wiki use has been determined
2. Tasks have been selected for use with the blog/wiki
3. Example blog/wiki sites have been selected for introduction
4. Tutorials have been developed to illustrate use
5. Necessary worksheets/handouts have been obtained or developed

Post-pedagogical Elements
1. A means to assess students has been developed
2. The blog/wiki will be locked when showcased

Pre-Blog/Pre-Wiki Student Considerations
All students will help compose and write the blog/posts/wiki articles, and add links or make any associated ongoing edits, comments, and replies. Also, you will need to identify group members who will be responsible for the following roles.

Post/Article Editor(s) _____

1. Keeping the language of the post/article linguistically correct (e.g. grammar, spelling, vocabulary use)
2. Following writing conventions (e.g. article flows, correct paragraph structure and formatting)

Citation Editor(s) _____

1. Curating resources
2. Ensuring sources are cited correctly
3. Confirming that all links and media work is as intended
4. Keeping the post/article plagiarism free
5. Maintaining use of copyright free content

Chief Editor(s) _____

1. Ensuring that the layout of the post/article is correct
2. Conducting a final proof of the post/article, tidying up, and correcting errors as necessary
3. Confirming that metadata is accurate, and providing tags
4. Establishing social media links, and the RSS feed

How to Write a Blog Post Resource Notes	
Post Title A title is chosen by students.	**Group Members** Student names are listed here.
Topic	Selected by students or provided by teacher.
Target	Students identify target audience, and relevant information regarding their topic.
Post Summary	Students write a short summary of their blog post to ensure that they are covering all details including their stance on the topic (positive or negative, and the reasons).
Post Outline	An outline of the post in point or sentence form needs to be given. Points of research can be added (e.g. links).
Supporting Media	Media choices to support the post need to be included (e.g. links, images, audio, videos, and infographics). All sources are cited.
The Post	The blog post is well composed.
Call to Action	A call to action is included (for example, asking readers to comment, or posing a question for readers to answer in the comments).
Proof, Tidy, Post, and Feed	The post is checked for accuracy (linguistic as well as factual) and appropriateness before it is posted. The post is also search engine optimized (SEO) with tags, working links, keywords, and accurate metadata. An RSS feed is available.

How to Write a Blog Post Handout	
Post Title	**Group members**

Topic	
Target	
Post Summary	
Post Outline	
Supporting Media	
Compose	
Proof, Tidy, Post, and Feed	

Peer Checklist – Blog Post	
Title	☐ Keywords from the post are used ☐ Written with a hook ☐ Succinct and focused on topic
Topic	☐ Encourages continued reading
Audience	☐ An intended target audience is identifiable
Post Outline	☐ Headings provide an overview ☐ Keywords used in sub-headings
Media	☐ Appropriate media used
Post	☐ Responds to task set
Introduction	☐ Succinct and focused on topic ☐ Key phrases can be used as metadata
Conclusion	☐ Useful, and provides a solution ☐ Creative and informative
Links	☐ Internal posts ☐ External sites ☐ Provide relevant/supporting information
Content	☐ Strong, and sums up the post very well ☐ Call to action included
Comments	☐ Readers can easily leave a comment
Proofing	☐ Plagiarism free ☐ RSS feed included ☐ No copyright infringement ☐ Sources cited correctly ☐ Tags added
Requires	☐ Error changes (linguistically/factually) ☐ More details ☐ Additional evidence
I Have	☐ Posted a comment ☐ Replied to a comment

How to Write a Wiki Article Resource Notes	
Article Title A title is chosen by students.	**Group Members** Student names are listed here.
Topic	Selected by students or provided by teacher.
Target Audience	Students identify target audience, and relevant information regarding their topic.
Article Summary	Students write a short summary of their article to ensure that they are covering all details, including their stance on the topic (positive or negative, and the reasons).
Article Outline	An outline of the article needs to be given. Points of research can be added (e.g. links).
Supporting Media	Media choices to support the article need to be included (e.g. links, images, audio, videos, and infographics). All sources are cited.
The Article	The article needs to be well composed, and perhaps follow the standard essay structure (introduction, body, and conclusion, with attention to paragraph structure – topic sentences, support sentences, and conclusive sentences).
Citations	Citations are included; article is plagiarism free.
Proof, Tidy, Post, and Feed	The article is checked for accuracy (linguistic as well as factual), and appropriateness. The post is also search engine optimized (SEO) with tags, working links, keywords, and accurate metadata. An RSS feed is available.

How to Write a Wiki Article Handout		
Article Title	**Group Members**	
Topic		
Target		
Article Summary		
Post Outline		
Supporting Media		
The Article		
Citations		
Proof, Tidy, Post, and Feed		

Peer Checklist – Wiki Article	
Title	☐ Keywords from the article are used
	☐ Succinct and focused on topic
Topic	☐ Article provides a significant contribution
Audience	☐ An intended target audience is identifiable
Post Outline	☐ Headings provide an overview
	☐ Keywords used in sub-headings
Media	☐ Appropriate media used to support article
Introduction	☐ Succinct and focused on topic
	☐ Written with a hook
Content	☐ Key phrases can be used as metadata
	☐ Responds to task set
	☐ Encourages continued reading
	☐ Useful and informative
Paragraphs	☐ Contain a single idea
	☐ Arguable claims supported
	☐ Evidence reflected on
Links	☐ Internal articles
	☐ External sites
	☐ Provide relevant/supporting information
Conclusion	☐ Strong, and sums up the article
Proofing	☐ Plagiarism free
	☐ Sources cited correctly
	☐ No copyright infringement
	☐ Tags added
	☐ RSS feed
I Have	☐ Made error changes
	☐ Added details
	☐ Provided additional supporting evidence

7. Resources List

7. Resources List

As sites continuously go down, merge, and emerge, perhaps only a small selection of all appropriate resource content should be presented here. An attempt at keeping the number of resources to a select few for each type also provides a sample that is both comprehensive and extensive, but not overwhelming. Like any other instructor resource list, individuals will be able to add to the content as they find material that is useful, creating their own bookmark list, and over time, come to curate a vast resource library tailored to their individual teaching and learning context. Each section of this list is broken down into applications that are mostly all freely available for use with Android or iOS devices, computers, or web-based platforms.

Teachers who wish to make notes, or to record any additional resources that they come across, can use the notes section at the end of this chapter.

The following content is covered:

- App creation
- Audio creation/editing
- Blogs
- Bookmarking
- Books
- Coding
- Comic strip generators
- Copyright
- Digital story creation
- Image resources
- Image editing
- Interactive whiteboards
- Mashups
- Media timelines
- Music resources
- Podcasting
- Podcatchers
- Presentations
- Publishing
- QR codes
- Rubrics
- Screencasting
- Storyboarding and scripting
- Story creation apps
- Video editing
- Video resources
- WebQuests
- Wikis

App Creation

Android – n/a
iOS – n/a
Computer – n/a
Web

Android Creator [free/paid] creates free Android apps without the need for programming knowledge.

AppMakr [free/paid] is a template based application creator that relies on drag and drop of elements for the development of no-coding required applications. It is available in a variety of languages.

Appy Pie [free/paid] relies on templates as well as drag and drop for users to begin creating their app. It requires no coding skills.

AppYourself [paid] is an app creation tool aimed at the business market.

Como DIY [paid] is a do-it-yourself app creation tool aimed to mostly target to businesses, and is available in a number of languages.

iBuildApp [paid] is a template driven app creator for iPhone and Android phones.

Audio Creation/Editing

Android

PCM Recorder [free] is a simple voice recorder.

Pocket WavePad [free] records edits and adds effects to audio.

TapeMachine [paid] is a graphical sound recorder and editor.

iOS

Pocket WavePad [free] records edits and adds effects to audio.

Voice Memos [paid] is voice recorder that allows multitasking.

Computer

Audacity [free] is an open source digital editing program available for Mac and PC which you can use to record, edit and mix narration and music.

Pocket WavePad [free] records, edits, and adds effects to audio for Mac.

GoldWave [free/paid] is a digital audio editor that provides simple recording as well as more sophisticated processing, restoration, enhancement, and conversion for Windows and Linux. A free version is available for evaluation purposes, after which a lifetime license can be purchased.

Web

Twistedwave [free] is a browser-based audio editor that can record or edit any audio file.

Blogs

Android

Blogaway [free] is a simple application to allow blogging on-the-go. It works with Blogger and allows for post creation, adding of photos, videos, multiple account management, saving of drafts, bookmarking, and a host of formatting options.

iOS

Disqus [free] is a commenting system that can be included in blogs as an add-on. The application provides an easy way to moderate comments and publish responses to keep engagement levels high.

TravelPod – Travel Blog [free] is a blogging application that works on- and offline, and is designed to be used while traveling.

Computer – n/a

Web

Blogger.com [free] will host your blog for free, and aside from being very easy to use, it allows some level of privacy so it can be suitable for use as a class blogging site. From a single account, you can create as many blogs as you wish and determine who is allowed to comment on the content.

BuzzSumo [paid] allows users to search for blog posts that have been highly shared across social media.

Edublogs.org [free] allows teachers to create and mange their own and students' websites. There is room for customization of design and the ability to add various media to this private and secure platform.

Kidblog.org [free] is an easy-to-use, safe, and secure publishing platform designed for students in grades K-12. There are a number of excellent features including privacy and password protection, and there is no need for student personal information to be collected, nor is there any advertising. It is free for up to fifty students per class.

WordPress.org [free] is one of the most popular blogging platforms in use today as it is open- source and is easily customizable. The downloadable software for self-hosting purposes is much more flexible than that available on the blogging platform.

Twitter [free] deserves a mention here as it is useful for microblogging (posting short frequent updates). It allows users to post and read short 140-character posts called 'tweets'.

Tumblr [free] is a blogging platform open to those over thirteen years of age, with most users using pen names over their real names when blogging. Users can post on their blog, follow others, and search posts. It is unique in that posts are divided into media types: text, photo, quote, link, chat, audio, and video.

Bookmarking

Android
> *Bookmark* [free] is a cross-platform app that allows for the syncing of bookmarks across different browsers and devices.
>
> *Delicious* [free] provides users with the ability to organize links to content on the internet that they would like to save, the ability to discover links, edit tags and comments, and also to explore content saved by friends.
>
> *Facebook Save* [free] is a built-in option for saving Facebook news content to read at a later date.
>
> *Instapaper* [free] provides an offline archiving solution for web pages, and it presents this content to be read in newspaper fashion. Content can be highlighted, and notes can be added while reading.
>
> *Pinterest* [free] allows users to pin posts (for example, web pages, images, and videos) and organize them around a common theme.
>
> *Pocket* [free] integrates with a large number of third party applications that allow for the building of bookmarks. Web pages, videos, images, and whatever else can be used offline for bookmarking. Archiving maintains the links but removes the content from offline availability.

iOS
> *Delicious* [free] allows users to save content from the internet (including web pages, blog posts, tweets, pictures, and video), and provides options for searching through others' collections of links.
>
> *Facebook Save* [free] is a built-in option for saving Facebook news content to read at a later date.
>
> *Instapaper* [free] provides an offline archiving solution for web pages and presents this content to be read in newspaper fashion. Content can be highlighted, and notes can be added while reading.

Pinterest [free] allows users to pin posts (for example, web pages, images, and videos) and organize them around a common theme.

Pocket [free] integrates with a large number of third party applications that allow for the building of bookmarks. Web pages, videos, images, and whatever else can be used offline for bookmarking. Archiving maintains the links but removes the content from offline availability.

Computer

EdwinSoft's UltimateDemon [paid] is link building software that helps to provide search engine optimization to a website.

Pinterest [free] allows users to pin posts (for example, web pages, images, and videos) and organize them around a common theme.

Pocket [free] integrates with a large number of third party applications that allow for the building of bookmarks. Web pages, videos, images, and whatever else can be used offline for bookmarking. Archiving maintains the links but removes the content from offline availability.

ReadKit [trial/paid] offers an Apple Mac curative and archiving platform for the content found in your other bookmarking applications (like Pocket and Instapaper) and RSS readers, and provides an extra level of organization to this content.

Web

Delicious [free] is a social bookmarking site that allows users to bookmark webpages to the internet instead of locally.

Facebook Save [free] is a built-in option for saving Facebook news content to read at a later date.

Instapaper [free] provides an offline archiving solution for web pages, and it presents this content to be read in newspaper fashion. Content can be highlighted, and notes can be added while reading.

OnlyWire [paid] works with WordPress and offers automatic submission of content to social networking and social bookmarking sites.

Pocket [free] integrates with a large number of third party applications that allow for the building of bookmarks. Web pages, videos, images, and whatever else can be used offline for bookmarking. Archiving maintains the links but removes the content from offline availability.

Books

Android

Wattpad Free Books [free] provides access to free stories and books written by aspiring authors.

iOS

Free Books – Ultimate Classics Library [free] features free access to 23,469 classic books.

Computer – n/a

Web

BookRix [free] allows access to thousands of books to read either online or to download as ebooks.

Children's Storybooks Online [free] provides a series of illustrated stories for all ages to read.

Coding

Android

Run Marco! [free] offers users the opportunity to play an adventure game while they learn to code. The application presents instructions using 'Blocky', which is the same as that used by the official Hour of Code tutorials.

Tynker [free] is an easy way for children to learn programming skills as they solve puzzles to learn concepts and build games, or control robots and drones. A number of templates are available for free.

iOS

Codea [paid] is a software development tool that uses the Lua programming language to teach users how to program.

Hopscotch [free] is an application that allows users to begin learning to code by making games similar to Angry Birds, and sharing them so others can play them.

ScratchJr [free] allows users to program their own interactive stories and games by snapping together graphical programming blocks. The application was inspired by the Scratch programming language.

Tynker [free] is an easy way for children to learn programming skills as they solve puzzles to learn concepts and build games, or control robots and drones. A number of templates are available for free.

Computer

Scratch [free] allows users to create stories, games, and animations using the Scratch programming language, and then share these with others. It is a project of the Lifelong Kindergarten Group at the MIT Media Lab.

Lightbot – Programming Puzzles [paid] is an OS X game-based application that allows players to use programming logic to solve levels. The app is also available for Android and iOS devices.

Web – n/a

Comic Strip Generators

Android

Comic Maker [free] creates comics from the photo gallery.

Comic Strip It! Lite [free] takes photos or use photo gallery images to create a comic.

iOS

Comic Life 3 [paid] turns photos into comic pages, or creates an entire comic from scratch using templates to build pages with speech balloons, comic lettering, and photo filters.

ToonTastic [free] is a wizard-based animated comic or cartoon creator.

Strip Designer [paid] is software for comic creation that uses camera, library, or Facebook photo options to create a comic.

Computer

Comic Creator [paid] is a basic template driven comic creator for use on a Windows computer.

Web

Pixton [free/paid] is an easy to use comprehensive online comic creator that supports narration, and offers a range of signup options from a free fun option to paid educator/business accounts.

MakeBeliefsComix [free] is a basic comic creator that uses black and white images over a four-panel comic strip. An iOS version is also available.

Toonlet [free] allows for anyone to create their own cartoon characters and web comics.

Toondoo [free] allows for the drag and drop creation of comic strips. An iOS version is also available.

Copyright

Android – n/a
iOS – n/a
Computer – n/a
Web

Creative Commons Licenses [free] gives detailed information regarding the various types of licensing afforded to creative commons, and the permissions that each license grants for the use specific works.

Image Codr [free] can assist learners and teachers alike in determining how a Flickr image can be used (as determined by the original photographer), and provides users with an automatically generated Creative Commons citation regarding the images use within digital projects.

Digital Story Creation

Android
Com-Phone Story Maker [free] combines audio, photos, and text to create stories while allowing for three different layers of audio.

WeVideo [free] is a web-based video editor that can mix images, text, video, and audio.

iOS
30hands [free] creates a story by adding narration to photos.

Magisto [free] uses a wizard to create a short video based on provided images or video content.

Splice [free/paid] combines photos, videos, music and narrations. Effects and transitions can be added.

WeVideo [free] is a web-based video editor that can mix images, text, video, and audio.

Computer
iMovie [paid] provides video creation and editing software that can create easily shareable content on a Mac. An iOS version is available.

Microsoft Photo Story 3 [free] for Windows lets you create slideshows from a wizard that includes audio, narration, and images.

Windows Movie Maker [free] for Windows operating systems is a video editing software application that allows for narration, audio, images, and video to be mixed and edited, and it comes with transitions and special effects.

Web
Animoto [paid] allows users to submit songs, choose a theme, add their photos, videos, and text to create a digital story that they can share.

Meograph [free] is a digital storytelling tool that relies on Google Earth to create map-based and timeline-based narrated stories.

WeVideo [free] is a web-based video editor that can mix images, text, video, and audio.

Image Resources

Android – n/a
iOS – n/a
Computer – n/a
Web

Cagle Cartoons [free] provides access to a number of political cartoons from around the world. The images are organized by topic with artists categorized by country.

Flickr Creative Commons [free] provides images that can be used for almost any educational project, as long as proper citation is followed

FreeFoto.com [free] has a photos area that is available under three licensing options: recognition, Creative Commons, and commercial.

Morguefile [free] provides a range of images that are copyright free, and are available for use with few or no restrictions.

Pics4Learning.com [free] is a website that provides safe and free images for educational uses. Images here are copyright-friendly and can be used for classrooms, multimedia projects, websites, videos, portfolios, or other projects.

PicSearch [free] allows you to search the internet for images, but be aware that the image may not be copyright-free, or that it may require permission to be used in projects or in any other educational contexts.

The Library of Congress Prints & Photographs Online Catalog [free] makes an attempt to ensure that as many of their images as possible are available online in a digital format.

Wikimedia [free] serves as a point from where all the images and video posted in Wikipedia can be viewed. Most of the images found here are either copyright-free or free for use with minimal restrictions.

Image Editing

Android

PicSay [free] can edit photos, overlay titles, and add special effects.

FX Camera [free] is a photo booth app that allows users to add various effects to photographs.

iOS

PhotoPad [free] can create, edit, and save vector illustrations. It can also work with photo library images.

ScreenChomp [free] allows you to share, explain, and markup images.

Computer

PhotoPad [paid] is an image editor for OS X.

PaintShop Pro [paid] is a comprehensive image editing package for Windows.

Web

Adobe Photoshop CC [paid] is a comprehensive cloud-based image editing package.

Phixr [free] is an online photo editor with various filters and effects, and it can connect to various social media sites.

FotoFlexer [free] is an online image editor offering a number of effects, distortions, and other features.

Pixlr [paid] is a comprehensive online photo editing app.

Interactive Whiteboards

Android

ExplainEverything [free] allows users to share their content by using an interactive screencasting whiteboard.

Interactive Whiteboard [free] is a virtual whiteboard that can be used for drawing or teaching various concepts as it allows for multiple finger input, straight line drawing mode, drawing move mode, and various other features.

PPT and Whiteboard Sharing [free] provides a way to share presentations, videos, and drawings in various settings including the classroom, the boardroom, and online meetings.

Whiteboard: Collaborative Draw [free] is a collaborative drawing application that allows real-time painting.

iOS

Doceri [trial/paid] combines screencasting, desktop control, and an interactive whiteboard in one application, with control through Airplay or through Mac or PC.

Educreations Interactive Whiteboard [free] is an interactive whiteboard and screencasting tool that allows annotation, animation, and narration of a number of content types.

Screenchomp [free] allows users to annotate pictures or to use the application as a whiteboard. Any work completed with the application can be saved automatically to the internet.

ShowMe Interactive Whiteboard [free] allows voice-over recording of whiteboard interactions so that tutorials can be created easily before being shared online.

Computer

Open Sakore [free] is open-source and it is dedicated to teacher and student use. It allows for insertion of multiple document types, along with annotation capabilities for commenting drawing and highlighting content.

Smoothboard Air [free] is a collaborative interactive whiteboard for multiple iPads and for Android tablets. It allows users to annotate desktop applications wirelessly through the use of a web browser.

Web

A Web Whiteboard [free] is a online whiteboard application that allows a number of devices (like computers, tablets, and smartphones), to draw sketches, and to collaborate with others around the globe.

Realtime Board [free] is a whiteboard in a browser that allows for collaboration among a number of users.

Twiddla [free] is a web-based meeting environment that allows users to mark up photos, graphics, and websites, or to just start out with a blank canvas.

Web Whiteboard [free] is a simple way to draw and write together online by creating an online whiteboard with a click, and sharing it live or by sending the link to others.

Mashups

Android

Edjing 5 DJ Music Mixer [free] not only transforms any android device into a turntable, but it provides access to a range of music libraries.

iOS

iMashup [paid] is a professional quality remixing app that allows users to create their own mashups and remixes.

Pacemaker [free] allows users to create and save mixes on an iPhone or iWatch, and to DJ live from iPad devices.

Computer

Mixxx [free] is an advanced open source DJ package that includes an extensive array of features for OS X and Windows.

Web

Mashstix [free] is a website with user submitted mashups available.

Media Timelines

Android

RWT Timelines [free] allows students to create a graphical representation of any event or process by displaying items sequentially along a line. The final product can be exported as a pdf, or saved to the device's camera roll.

Timeline [free] allows users to create timelines and associate them with colors, and to view multiple timelines together. It is a useful reference tool for remembering dates.

iOS

TimelineBuilder [paid] allows users to create custom timelines with images and text with unique beginning and end dates.

Timeline Maker [free] provides an easy way to display a series of events in a chronological order.

Computer

Edraw Timeline Maker [paid] is a tool that makes it simple to create a professional looking timeline, history, schedule, time table, or project plan diagram from scratch.

TimelineMaker [paid] provides a simplified timeline charting tool aimed at project planners, and business professionals, and those in educational contexts.

Web

Capzles [free] allows users to create rich multimedia experiences from videos, photos, music, blogs, and documents by integrating these into a timeline of sequential events, and then share them on various social media platforms.

Hstry [free] is specifically designed for the education sector, and it allows teachers and students to create interactive timelines for assignments and online sharing.

OurStory [free] offers a means for creating story-based timelines with pictures.

Timeline [free] from *readwritethink* allows students of all ages to easily create a graphical representation of related items or events in sequential order and display them along a line using various images and text.

TimeGlider [free] is a web-based timeline project creator that allows zooming and panning across timelines. Users are able to set the size of events as they relate to importance.

Tiki-Toki [free/paid] is a web-based timeline editor that allows viewing of timelines in 3D, and it allows for the integration of images and videos.

WhenInTime [free] is a web application for creating and sharing media-based timelines.

Music Resources

Android

FindSounds [free] can be used to search the internet for sounds that can then be saved as ringtones, notifications, or alarms.

Shazam [free] allows Android device users to identify the music playing around them, as well as discover song lyrics, and other music related information and tracks.

iOS

Shazam [free] allows iOS device users to identify the music playing around them, as well as discover song lyrics, and other music related information and tracks.

Computer – n/a

Web

300 Monks [free] provides a comprehensive source of royalty free music.

ccMixter [free] is a free music site that is community based and promotes a remix culture. *A cappella* and remix tracks licensed under Creative Commons are available for download and use in creative works.

FMA (Free Music Archive) [free] provides access to a range of free music based on a wide variety of genre. The music is offered free under various licenses for use.

Find Sounds [free] is a long-running service that can be used to search the internet for various sounds that can then be incorporated into various projects.

FreePlay Music [free] is a service that searches the internet for free music that can be used in YouTube videos and other projects.

Podcasting

Android

Podomatic Podcast & Mix Player [free] provides access to a wide variety of podcasts, listening in offline mode, and features such as a dynamic social feed so you can see the podcasts Facebook friends follow and like.

iOS

PodOmatic Podcast Player [free] provides access to a wide variety of podcasts, listening in offline mode, and features such as a dynamic social feed so you can see the podcasts Facebook friends follow and like.

Computer

Audacity [free] is a free multi-track audio recorder and editor with some very powerful features that include those for adding effects to files and conducting analysis of the audio recorded.

iTunes [free] offers media on demand and a way to organize and enjoy music, movies, and TV shows, as well as accessing and subscribing to podcasts and screencasts.

LoudBlog [free] is a Content Management System (CMS) for podcasts. This program automatically generates skinnable websites and RSS-feeds for audio and video podcasts, including provision for show notes and links.

PodcastGenerator [free] is an open source content management system for podcast publishing. It provides a comprehensive range of tools to manage all aspects of podcast publishing.

PodProducer [free] allows for the recording of voice and the adding of effects.

Web

ESLPod [free] provides a range of podcast content tailored to second-language learners of English from specific topics through to test-taking guides.

FeedForAll [free] allows for the creation, editing, and publishing of RSS feeds.

Feedity [free] is an online tool for creating an RSS feed for any web page, with an option to upgrade to a premium account that offers additional features.

FETCHRSS: RSS Generator [free] is an online RSS feed generator, that can create a feed out of almost any web page, automatically updates the RSS feed when new content is added to the web page, and generates an RSS for a social networking site.

OPML Viewer [free] allows users to view the contents of outline processor markup language (OPML) files.

Podcast Alley [free] is the place to go if you are interested in podcasts, want to gain access to the top podcasts, and want to find out the latest news about podcasts.

Pod Gallery [free] is a podcasting website where podcasters can share their episodes, and where listeners can subscribe.

QT-ESL Podcasts [free] provides a range of podcasts that cover oral grammar practice and includes scripts and worksheets.

SoundCloud [free] is a social sound platform where anyone is able to create and share audio.

Podcatchers

Android

Podcast Player [free] provides a range of podcast discovery options and tools, along with a range of features including a sleep timer, video support, intelligent silence skip and volume boost, as well as support for tablet, Chromecast, and Android Wear.

Podcast Republic [free] is an application that is ad-supported. It offers a variety of features from podcast discovery and automatic downloading through to storage management, sleep timer, and car mode. Support is also included from Chromecast and Android Wear.

Pocket Casts [paid] shows subscribed podcasts in a tile format, with easy sorting and categorization functions. Video podcast is also supported, along with auto-download and cleanup of downloaded and played episodes to save on storage space. Several features allow it to stand out, including a sleep timer as well as its cross-platform nature that grants it the ability to sync between multiple devices and mobile operating systems.

iOS

Overcast*: Podcast Player* [free] provides a combination of powerful audio and podcast management features. The application comes with a wide variety of features that allow it to download episodes, send notifications of new episodes, and play content offline or by streaming. It can also normalize speech levels, and speed through gaps and silence in podcasts.

Castro*: High Fidelty Podcasts* [free] is a simple and easy to use podcatcher. It provides a simple design with automatic episode download, dynamic storage management, along with episode streaming.

Pocket Casts [paid] shows subscribed podcasts in a tile format, with easy sorting and categorization functions. Video podcast is also supported, along with auto-download and cleanup of downloaded and played episodes to save on storage space. Several features allow it to stand out, including a sleep timer as well as its cross-platform nature that grants it the ability to sync between multiple devices and mobile operating systems.

Computer

gPodder [free] is an open source media aggregator and podcast client. It is able to store information in the cloud on which shows you have listened to, and it allows for the local installation of the client for download of content.

iTunes [free] is a comprehensive media aggregator that provides comprehensive support for media management, the audio and video playback of local media, podcast search and subscription, along with automatic downloads, syncing and streaming, and many other features.

Juice [free] is a long-standing cross platform no-frills podcast aggregator that is open source, and specifically designed to manage podcasts. Features include auto cleanup, centralized feed management, and for Windows users, accessibility options for the blind and visually impaired.

Web

Cloud Caster [free] is a web-based podcaster which works across all mobile devices. It syncs progress and playlists across platforms, and provides search and support for audio and video podcasts.

Presentations

Android

Glogster [free] allows students using an Android-based device to create online multimedia posters, or Glogs, from a combination of media types (from audio, graphic, to video), and hyperlinks.

Google Slides [free] allows Android device users with a Google account a means of creating, editing, and collaborating with others on presentations.

LinkedIn SlideShare [free] allows Android device users the ability to search and explore for a variety of presentations, infographics, and documents on topics of their interest.

Microsoft PowerPoint [free] allows users to view PowerPoint presentations on their device for free, and to make edits and changes on the go.

iOS

Glogster [free] allows students using an iOS device to create online multimedia posters, or Glogs, from a combination of media types (from audio, graphic, to video), and hyperlinks.

Google Slides [free] allows iOS device users with a Google account a means of creating, editing, and collaborating with others on presentations.

Keynote [free] is a powerful presentation app that allows users to develop comprehensive presentations with animations, transitions, and multimedia elements.

LinkedIn SlideShare [free] allows iOS device users the ability to search and explore for a variety of presentations, infographics, and documents on topics of their interest.

Microsoft PowerPoint [free] allows users to view PowerPoint presentations on their device for free, and to make edits and changes on the go.

Computer

Microsoft PowerPoint [paid] is a comprehensive presentation software application, and is perhaps the most used and recognizable.

Keynote [free] is a powerful presentation app that allows users to develop comprehensive presentations with animations, transitions, and multimedia elements.

Web

Bunkr [free] is a presentation tool that displays any online content including social media posts, images, videos, audio, articles, and files.

Glogster [free] allows students to create online multimedia posters, or Glogs, from a combination of media types (from audio, graphic, to video), and hyperlinks.

Google Slides [free] allows those with a Google account, a means of creating, editing, and collaborating with others on presentations.

LinkedIn SlideShare [free] allows users to search for presentations, infographics, documents and other items on topics of their interest.

Microsoft PowerPoint Online [free] extends the Microsoft PowerPoint experience to the web browser with OneDrive integration, and allows users to create, edit, and view files on the go.

Prezi [free] is a visually oriented presentation packaged that also allows users to upload PowerPoint slides, and customize them, or use a variety of their own images, text, audio, and video.

Slidebean [free] offers a one-click presentation development system that incorporates a variety of templates into the design of presentations.

Slides [free] is a place for creating, presenting, and sharing slide decks.

Swipe [free] allows users to share a presentation link with anyone across any device, and it allows viewers to interact with the presentation on several levels, from collaboration through to taking polls.

VoiceThread [free] allows users to import various media such as images, PowerPoints, and PDFs. It provides a means of making audio or video recordings concerning those media artifacts, and it also allows other users to reply to the initial comments, by audio or video means, as the presentation progresses.

Publishing

Android

Book Creator Free [free] offers a simple means of creating a variety of ebooks including picture books, comic and photo books, and journals and textbooks. It allows for the use of images, narration, texts, annotations and drawings.

Book Writer Free [free] is a simple book creation application that allows users to share their content with others.

My Story Builder [free] is a simple, 'suitable for children', book editor.

Scribble: Kids Book Maker [paid] is an application that allows children to write, illustrate, and publish their own comprehensive stories in a range of formations including video export. It contains a series of story starters, stickers, and backgrounds to help them work on creating stories from the start.

iOS

Book Creator Free [free] offers a simple means of creating a variety of ebooks including picture books, comic and photo books, and journals and textbooks. It allows for the use of images, narration, texts, annotations and drawings.

Creative Book Builder [paid] is a professional ebook editor and generator which can also extend the utility of ebooks through the use of a range of widgets.

Demibooks Composer Pro [free] builds interactive books with animation, audio, images, and effects.

Scribble Press – Creative Book Maker for Kids [paid] contains a series of story starters, stickers and backgrounds to help get young kids working on creating stories that can be turned into ebooks.

Computer

Android Book App Maker [paid] provides users with the ability to turn content into a flip-book app.

iBooks Author [free] provides a series of templates and styles to assist in the development of ebooks for the iBook store.

Kotobee [free] provides free software to assist in the creation of ebooks and libraries for a range of platforms.

Web

Blurb [paid] is just one of many online services that can assist in the creation of ebooks.

QR Codes

Android

I-nigma QR & Barcode Scanner (free) is a versatile barcode and QR code reader that can scan a multitude of codes and share these codes as well.

QR Code Reader (free) is a simple QR Code and product barcode scanner.

QR Droid Code Scanner (free) is a powerful barcode, QR code, and Data Matrix scanner that offers multi-language support.

iOS

Bakodo – Barcode Scanner and QR Barcode Reader (free) scans all types of QR codes and barcodes.

QR Reader for iPhone (free) scans a variety of codes including QR codes and barcodes, and features auto-detect scanning.

QRafter – QR Code and Barcode Reader and Generator (free) is a two-dimensional barcode scanner for iOS. Along with a variety of useful features, it can scan and generate QR codes.

Computer

CodeTwo QR Code Desktop Reader (free) allows users to scan QR codes directly from their screen onto their desktop. Users select the QR code to be read by selecting the area with a QR code using their mouse.

QR-Code Studio (free) is for Mac and Windows computers. The QR code maker software is freeware.

Web

QR Code Generator (free) creates QR codes, in a limited number of formats, for free.

QR Stuff QR Code Generator (free) creates QR codes from a various types of data such as website URLs, image files, PDF files, and so on, with static and dynamic embedding options.

The QR Code Generator (free) allows for the free scan and generation of QR codes for a variety of uses.

Rubrics

Android

Daily Rubric: Any Curriculum [free] allows teachers to create and use rubrics from their Android device. Rubrics can be designed from curriculum outcomes, or based on the pre-loaded Common Core Standards.

iOS

Easy Assessment [paid] offers a means to capture and assess performance based on custom created rubrics, scale, or criteria.

Rubrics [paid] allows instructors to track student performance and produce reports based on custom rubrics and grading options.

Computer – n/a

Web

Kathy Shrock's Guide to Everything: Assessment and Rubrics [free] provides access to a wide range of rubrics to help guide assessment of students.

iRubric [free] is a website where instructors can create their own rubrics, or they can build off those made available from other instructors.

RubiStar [free] allows instructors to create their own rubrics using templates designed for core subjects as well as art, music, and multimedia.

Screencasting

Android
AZ Screen Recorder [free] is a screen recording application that offers several features, including the ability to capture the front camera as well as screen recording. It also provides video trimming.

ilos Screen Recorder [free] is a simple application that records the screen and provides audio capture as well.

Telecine [free] is an open source application that allows screen recording through the use of overlays.

iOS
Doceri [trial/paid] combines screencasting, desktop control, and an interactive whiteboard in one application, with control through Airplay or through Mac or PC.

Educreations Interactive Whiteboard [free] is an interactive whiteboard and screencasting tool that allows annotation, animation, and narration of a number of content types.

Screenchomp [free] allows users to annotate pictures or to use the application as a whiteboard. Any work completed with the application can be saved automatically to the internet.

Computer
ilos screen recorder [free] automatically uploads content to their servers for storage and playback.

Screencast-O-Matic [free] offers fifteen minutes of recording time for free, both for screen and webcam, and allows users to save to places such as YouTube or as a video file.

TechSmith Camtasia Studio [free trial] is a comprehensive screen recording application that allows for audio and webcam capture as well as highlighting, adding media, and editing of recordings.

Web – n/a

Storyboarding and Scripting

Android
Ray Story Board [free] is a simple storyboard creator that lets users build storyboards from photos or gallery images, create

multiple storyboards, and animate them using a slideshow feature.

Storyboard Studio [paid] is a mobile storyboarding writing tool that is suitable for artists and non-artists alike.

iOS

Penultimate [free] provides a natural feel of writing and sketching on paper, and connects to Evernote.

Storyboard Composer [paid] is a mobile storyboard previsualiztion composer for animators, art directors, film students, film directors, or anyone who would like to visualize their story.

Computer

FrameForge Previz Studio [paid] allows users to develop and previsualize films, TV shows, commercials, or similar projects at a professional level.

Storyboardpro [paid] is professional level software that combines drawing and animation tools with camera controls.

StoryBoard Quick Studio [paid] allows for the fast creation of storyboards with QuickShots, has a print-to-sketch feature, and comes with a series of character poses for integration into storylines.

Web

Google Docs [free] can be used, along with any note-taking or document editor, as a make-shift storyboard by integrating photos or pictures into the document to outline a process or the actions for a story. It is also available as an Android and iOS app.

StoryboardThat [free trial] offers an edition that allows educators to build diagrams, and visualize workflow. It features a drag and drop interface and an extensive image library.

Story Creation Apps

Android

StoryMaker 1 [free] provides a means of creating stories using templates and overlays, and the possibility of using audio, photos, or video.

Storehouse [free] allows users to share a collection of photos in a collage or album, or by telling a story that links the photos.

iOS

StoryKit [free] allows for the creation of an electronic storybook through the use of images, simple drawings, recording of sound, and by the addition of text.

Storyrobe [paid] makes photo-based slideshows with voice recording.

FotoBabble [free] adds audio to a photo to make a talking postcard.

Sock Puppets [free] lets users create lip-synced videos with characters. Various puppets, props, scenery, and backgrounds can be used.

Computer

Cartoon Story Maker 1.1 [free] is a simple program that creates 2D cartoon stories with conversations, dialogs (recorded and/or speech bubble), and various backgrounds.

StoryMaker [free/trial] is game-based software that asks for parts of speech (such as nouns, verbs, adjectives), and these are then inserted into a story with sometimes comical results. Educators can edit and customize aspects of the aspects of the program for their context. Backgrounds can be imported, but character templates are built in.

Web

Littlebirdtales [free] provides younger learners the ability to create digital storybooks.

Pixton [free/paid] is a visual writing tool that allows users to make a comic using images, clipart backgrounds and artwork, as well as speech bubbles.

Storynet.org [free] is a website that aims at connecting people to and through storytelling.

StoryJumper [free] allows users to create illustrated storybooks from scratch or from existing templates.

Video Editing

Android

VideoShow – Video Editor [free] is an all-in-one video editor and slideshow producer that provides music, themes, filters, emojis, as well as text input.

VidTrim [free] is a video editor and organizer that allows the trimming, editing, and saving of videos.

VivaVideo: Free Video Editor [free] is a comprehensive video editor and movie maker that facilitates the creation of video-based stories.

WeVideo [free] is a comprehensive and easy to use video editor that can mix images, text, video, and audio.

iOS

iMovie [paid] is video creation and editing software that can create easily shareable content.

Splice [free] is a video editor that adds music and effects to images and videos with narration. It includes access to free songs, sound effects, text overlays, transitions, filters, and various editing tools.

ReelDirector II [paid] is a full-featured video editing app.

WeVideo [free] is an easy to use and comprehensive video editor that can mix audio, images, text, and audio.

Computer

Windows Movie Maker [free] is a video editing software application that allows for narration, audio, images, and video to be mixed and edited with transitions and special effects.

Web

Video Toolbox [free] is an online video editing and conversion tool.

WeVideo [free] is a comprehensive and easy to use web-based video editor that can mix images, text, video, and audio together to form a compelling story.

Video Resources

Android

TED [free] provides more than 2,000 TED talks from various people by topic and mood, and on a variety of topics.

Vimeo [free] is a variety of videos are available across a wide variety of topics and genres, with users having the ability to upload their own content as well.

YouTube [free] allows for editing and uploading of videos, where one can subscribe to various channels that offer a wide variety of videos on various topics and genres.

iOS

TED [free] provides more than 2,000 TED talks from various people by topic and mood, and on a variety of topics.

Vimeo [free] provides a variety of videos which are available across a wide variety of topics and genres. Users are able to upload their own content as well.

YouTube [free] allows for editing and uploading of videos, where once can subscribe to various channels that offer a wide variety of videos on various topics and genres.

Computer – n/a

Web

Clipcanvas [free] allows for the download of 600,000 royalty free HD and 4K video and film clips.

Mazwai [free] maintains a collection of free to use HD video clips and footage, and some unique time-lapse and slow motion video footages that are provided under the Creative Commons Attribution license if used commercially.

Motion Backgrounds for Free [free] is a place to download professional quality motion backgrounds and video footage.

Motion Elements [free] is a good source for premium stock videos, offering around 400 videos for free, as well as free After Effects templates.

Neo's Clip Archive [free] offers nearly 3,500 free video clips sorted by 25 categories free for use for personal, non-commercial purposes.

Pexels Videos [free] brings under one roof a video library of Creative Commons Zero licensed stock videos from a variety of different sources.

SaveTube [free] allows users to rip YouTube videos to their local computer in various audio or video-based formats.

Savevideo.me [free] allows users to rip videos from a variety of sites to their local computer.

TeacherTube [free] is an online resource that helps users to view and share videos, photos, audio, and documents on almost any topic.

WebQuests

Android – n/a
iOS – n/a
Computer – n/a
Web

Building a WebQuest [free] is a comprehensive overview of the template to follow when there is a need to construct a WebQuest.

Having Fun with Reading [free] is a WebQuest for college and adult level learners of English, where learners interact with texts and complete activities that promote cooperative and collaborative learning along with reading narrative comprehension skills.

Idioms in Your Pocket [free] is a WebQuest that is designed for high school and adult ESL students, and it allows them to discover the various meanings of English idioms.

OneStopEnglish WebQuests [free] provides a selection of WebQuests covering major holidays.

Pre-Writing Your WebQuest [free] provides prompts for users to complete in order to develop a WebQuest.

QuestGarden [free/paid] is a site designed by Bernie Dodge, the creator of WebQuests, for use by pre- and in-service teachers, professional developers, other educators, and those who work with them. The site provides hosting and template creation of WebQuests that then become searchable.

Using WebQuests to Teach English [free] is a WebQuest that can be used to teach teachers about WebQuests.

WebQuestDirect [free] is described as the world's largest searchable directory of WebQuest reviews.

WebQuest.Org [free] provides comprehensive information pertaining to the WebQuest model, and is run by Bernie Dodge, the creator of WebQuests.

Zunal [free/paid] is a site for educators to create, host, and then share their WebQuests with others.

Wikis

Android

EveryWiki: Wikipedia++ [free] aims to provide access to many wikis from a central application.

wikiHow [free] is the application associated with the leading how-to-guide wikiHow. It allows for searching of the wiki to find step-by-step instructions on how to complete almost any task.

iOS

Hack My Life – Life Hack Wiki [free] is an application that seeks to provide access to all possible life hacks. A life hack is a strategy or technique that can be used or adopted to allow for better time management or for getting more out of everyday activities.

Lyrically [free] offers access to a list of song lyrics curated by fans. Searches can be undertaken by track, artist, or by song, and there is support for in-app purchases.

Computer

DokuWiki [free] is a PHP based highly customizable and fully extensible wiki software platform. The advantage is that it requires no databases as all the data is stored in plain text, and for this reason, it is very popular and used by many sites. It has a variety of useful features, from locking to avoid edits through to a spam blacklist.

MediaWiki [free] is open-source and it is the wiki software used by Wikipedia. It is available in a number of languages, released under a general public license (GPL), and written in PHP: Hypertext Preprocessor (PHP) a server-side scripting language. There are many extensions and plugins available for free, including a what-you-see-is-what-you-get (WYSIWYG) editor.

Web

PBworks [free] (formerly PBwiki) is a real-time collaborative editing system with several solutions including one for educators. It offers a single workspace, where student accounts can be created without email addresses, and easy editing without the need for coding.

PmWiki [free] is a wiki tool that gives user-access control over individual pages, so they can be set for access by specific people with it being possible to set different passwords for each page.

The software also allows for navigation trails through individual sections, insertion of tables, and provides a printable layout.

Wikidot [free] offers members the ability to create a wiki-based website with forums, where they can create a community, or publish and share documents and content.

Wikispaces [free] is a wiki hosting service that provides educators with a means to monitor student progress in real time and the ability to easily create projects and assign them to students, as well as editing tools and a social newsfeed.

Teacher Notes

Android

iOS

Computer

Web

References

Ahmad, S. Z. (2012). The effect of WebQuests on EFL students' critical reading. *First International Conference of the Egyptian Association for Curriculum and Instruction*. September 5-6. Suez, Egypt.

Al Khateeb, A. A. (2013). Wikis in EFL writing classes in Saudi Arabia: Identifying instructors' reflections on merits, demerits and implementation. *Teaching English with Technology, 13*(4), 3-22.

Al-Kilidar, H. & Johnson, C. (2009). The use of wikispace in engingeeering education. In *Engineering the Curriculum: Proceedings of the 20th Annual Conference for the Australasian Association for Engineering Education*. December 6-9. Adelaide, Australia.

Ali, A. D. (2016). Effectiveness of Using Screencast Feedback on EFL Students' Writing and Perception. *English Language Teaching, 9*(8), 106-121.

Alshumaimeri, Y. A., & Almasri, M. M. (2012). The Effects of Using Webquests on reading comprehension performance of Saudi EFL students. *TOJET: The Turkish Online Journal of Educational Technology, 11*(4), 295-306.

Akasha, O. (2011). Voicethread as a good tool to motivate ELLs and much more. In M. Koehler & P. Mishra (eds.), *Proceedings of Society for Information Technology & Teacher Education International Conference 2011* (pp. 3123-3127). Chesapeake, VA: Association for the Advancement of Computing in Education (AACE).

Arauz, P. E. (2013). Inquiry-based learning in an English as a foreign language class: A Proposal. *Revista De Lenguas Modernas, 19*. 479-485.

Aydin, Z., & Yildiz, S. (2014). Using wikis to promote collaborative EFL writing. *Language Learning & Technology, 18*(1), 160-180.

Benjamin, J. Y. (2003, January 08). A checklist for evaluating WebQuests. *Tech & Learning*. Retrieved from http://www.techlearning.com/news/0002/a-checklist-for-evaluating-webquests/55765

Burden, K. & Atkinson, S. (2008). Evaluating pedagogical 'affordances' of media sharing Web 2.0 technologies: A case study. In Hello! Where are you in the landscape of educational technology? *ascilite Melbourne 2008*.

Bush, L. (2009). Viva VoiceThread: Integrating a web 2.0 Tool in the additional language classroom In I. Gibson, R. Weber, K. McFerring, R. Carlsen & D. Willis (Eds.), *Proceedings of Society for Information Technology & Teacher Education International Conference 2009* (pp. 3247-3250). Chesapeake, VA: Association for the Advancement of Computing in Education (AACE).

Campbell, A. P. (2003). Weblogs for use with ESL classes. *The Internet TESOL Journal, IX*(2). Retrieved from http://iteslj.org/Techniques/Campbell-Weblogs.html

Cassinelli, C. (2016). Voicethread. *Voicethread 4 Education*. Retrieved from http://voicethread4education.wikispaces.com

Chou, I. C. (2014). Situated learning: Learn to tell English stories. *Journal of Education and Training Studies, 2*(4), 113-118.

Chuo, T. W. I. (2007). The effects of the WebQuest writing instruction program on EFL learners' writing performance, writing apprehension and perception. *TESL-EJ, 11*(3), 1-27.

Croome, J. (2011). *12 easy steps to the making of a book trailer*. Retrieved from http://www.thebookdesigner.com/2011/05/12-easy-steps-to-the-making-of-a-book-trailer/

Dodge, B. (2001). Five rules for writing a great WebQuest. *Learning & Leading with Technology, 28*(8), 6-9.

Dodge, B. (2015). *What is a WebQuest?* Retrieved from http://webquest.org

Doyle, B. (2015). *How to create an Animoto book trailer*. Retrieved from https://www.youtube.com/watch?v=mUWjNHs7c5c

Dyck, B. (2007). VoiceThread: Capturing and sharing student voice with an online twist. *EducationWorld*. Retrieved from http://www.educationworld.com/a_tech/columnists/dyck/dyck019.shtml

EBC (2004). *Concept to classroom*. Retrieved from http://www.thirteen.org/edonline/concept2class/webquests/index.html

Elwood, S. (2010). Digital storytelling: Strategies using VoiceThread. In D. Gibson & B. Dodge (Eds.), *Proceedings of Society for Information & Teacher Education International Conference* 2010 (pp. 1075-1079). Chesapeake, VA: Association for the Advancement of Computing in Education (AACE).

Ferriter, B. (2010). Voicethread. *Digitally Speaking*. Retrieved from http://digitallyspeaking.pbworks.com/Voicethread

FMA. *(2016). free music archive*. Retrieved from http://freemusicarchive.org/

Foord, D. (2016). Resources – Social software. *A6 Training & Consultancy Ltd*. Retrieved from http://www.a6training.co.uk/resources_Social_Software.php

Gablenick, F., MacGregor, J., Matthews, R., & Smith, B. L. (1990). Learning communitities: Creating connections among students, faculty, and disciplines. New Directions for Teaching and Learning, 41 (Spring). San Francisco, USA: Jossey-Bass.

Gaille, B. (2013). *How many Blogs are on the Internet?* WPVirtuoso. Retrieved from http://www.wpvirtuoso.com/how-many-blogs-are-on-the-internet/

Gillis, A., Luthin, K., Parette, H.P., & Blum, C. (2012). Using VoiceThread to create meaningful receptive and expressive learning activities for young children. *Early Childhood Education 40(4)*, 203--211.

Godwin-Jones, B. Blog and Wikis: Environments for online collaboration. *Language Learning & Technology, 7*(2), 12-16.

Goins, J. (2016). *Why most book trailers are awful and how yours can be different*. Retrieved from http://goinswriter.com/book-trailer

Gunelius, S. (2016). What is a blog? *Abouttech*. Retrieved from http://weblogs.about.com/od/startingablog/p/WhatIsABlog.htm

Hacker, P. (2010). Using VoiceThread to give students a voice outside the classroom. *The Chronicle of Higher Education*. Retrieved from http://chronicle.com/blogs/profhacker/using-voicethread-to-give-students-a-voice-outside-the-classroom/26367

Harclerode, M. (n.d.). *Book trailers for readers*. Retrieved from http://www.booktrailersforreaders.com/How+to+make+a+book+trailer

Horvath, J. (2008). Hungarian university students' Blogs in EFL: Shaping language and social connections. *TESL-EJ, 12*(4), 1-9.

Hoskins Sakamoto, B. (2010). High tech ideas for low tech classrooms: VoiceThread. *Teaching Village*. Retrieved from http://www.teachingvillage.org/2010/05/23/high-tech-ideas-for-low-tech-classrooms-voicethread

Howland, J., Jonassen, D., & Marra, R. (2012). *Meaningful learning with technology, 4th ed.* Boston, MA: Pearson.

Hughes, H. (2012). Introduction to flipping the college classroom. In T. Amiel & B. Wilson (Eds.), *Proceedings of EdMedia: World Conference on Educational Media and Technology 2012* (pp. 2434-2438). Association for the Advancement of Computing in Education (AACE).

James, B. Wide open spaces: Wikis ready or not. EDUCAUSE Review, 39(5), 36, 38, 40, 42, 44-46, 48.

Jatkowski Homuth, J., & Piippo, A. (2012). Using wikis in the ESL classroom. In J. M. Perren, D. Ouano Perren, & T. Dowling (Eds.)., *"Serving for a Better World" Selected Proceedings of the 2012 Michigan Teachers of English to Speakers of Other Languages Conference*. October 12-13, Livonia. Michigan, USA.

JLG (2016). *What makes a good book trailer*. Retrieved from https://www.youtube.com/watch?v=wYQCaolRQ4g

Jordan, A., Carlile, O., & Stack, A. (2008). *Approaches to learning: A guide for teachers*. Berkshire: McGraw-Hill, Open University Press.

Keen, A. (2008). *The cult of the amateur: How today's internet is killing our culture*. New York: Nicholas Brealey Publishing.

Kent, D. B. (2015). iPadagogy: Using mobile devices to extend language learning strategies. *The English Connection, 19*(1), 27-30.

Kent, D. B. (2016). Analysis of a Korea-based language teacher organization public social networking service. *International Journal of Contents, 12*(2), 66-74.

Koenraad, T.L., & Westhoff, G. J. (2003). Can you tell a LanguageQuest when you see one?: Design criteria for TalenQuests. *Conference of the European Association for Computer Assisted Language Learning*. September 3-6. University of Limerick, Ireland.

Kocoglu, Z. (2010). WebQuests in EFL reading/writing classroom. *Innovation and Creativity in Education, 2*(2), 3524-3527.

Lamb, H. (2004). My brilliant future: Wikis in classrooms. Kairosnews. Retrieved from http://kairosnews.org/node/3794

Leuf, B., & Cunningham, W. (2002). *What is a Wiki*. Retrieved from http://www.wiki.org/wiki.cgi?WhatIsWiki

Lewis, T., Burks, B., Shumack, K., & Simmons, K. (2014). VoiceThread: Instructional improvement through objective feedback. In M. Searson & M. Ochoa (Eds.), *Proceedings of Society for Information Technology & Teacher Education International Conference 2014* (pp. 2907-2910). Chesapeake, VA: Association for the Advancement of Computing in Education (AACE).

Lincoln, L. (2014). *Book trailer tutorial using (Windows) Movie Maker*. Retrieved from https://www.youtube.com/watch?v=t9 e-4xumP4A

Lund, A., & Smordal, O. (2006). Is there space for the teacher in a wiki? *Proceedings of the International Symposium on Wikis*, 37-46.

Mak, B., & Coniam, D. (2008). Using wikis to enhance and develop writing skills among secondary school students in Hong Kong. *System, 36*(3), 437-455.

March, T. (2004). New needs, new curriculum. *Educational Leadership, 61*(4), 42-47.

Matsil, N. (2015). *How to make a book trailer for free (That looks professional)*. Retrieved from https://www.powtoon.com/blog/ book-trailer-free-professional/

Mazwai. (2016). *Mazwai*. Retrieved from http://mazwai.com

McLoughlin, C., & Lee, M. W. (2007). Social software and participatory learning: Pedagogical choices with technology affordances in the Web 2.0 era. ICT: Providing choices for learners and learning. *Proceedings ascilite Singapore 2007*. Centre for Educational Development, Nanyang Technological University. December 2-5, Singapore.

Merholz, P. (1999). *PeterMe.com*. Retrieved from https://web.archive.org/web/19991013021124/http://peterme.c om/index.html

Moore, A. J., Gillet, M. R., & Steele, M. D., (2014). Fostering student engagement with the flip. *The Mathematics Teacher 107*(6), 420-425.

Mossberger, K., Tolbert, C. J., & Stansbury, M. (2003). *Virtual inequality: Beyond the digital divide*. USA: Georgetown University Press.

Najafi, S. (2013). *Fantastic book trailers and the reasons they are so good*. Retrieved from http://therumpus.net/2013/06/fantastic-book-trailers-and-the-reasons-theyre-so-good/

Nassaji, H., & Cummings, A. (2000). What's in a ZPD? A case study of a young ESL student and teacher interacting through dialogue journals. *Language Teaching Research, 4*(2), 95-121.

Nations, D. The Wiki list. *Abouttech*. Retrieved from http://webtrends.about.com/od/wikilists/tp/list_of_wiki_sites.htm

Nicholsan, M. (2013). Flipping the classroom with VoiceThread discussions. In T. Bastianes & G. Marks (Eds.), *Proceedings of E-Learn: World Conference on E-Learning in Corporate, Government, Healthcare, and Higher Education* 2013 (pp. 1263-1264). Chesapeake, VA: Association for the Advancement of Computing in Education (AACE).

Pacansky-Brock, M. (2013). *How to humanize your online class with VoiceThread*. Imprint: Smashwords Edition.

Pallos, H. & Pallos, L. (2011). Evaluation of Voicethread technology to improve Japanese graduate students presentation skills in English in a blended learning environment. In S. Barton, J. Hedberg & K. Suzuki (Eds.), *Proceedings of Global Learn 2011* (p. 1078). AACE.

Pederson, R. (2013). Situated learning: Rethinking a ubiquitous theory. *The Journal of Asia TEFL, 9*(2), 123-148.

Penn, J. (2013). *Book Trailers: 11 Steps to make your own*. Retrieved from http://www.thecreativepenn.com/2008/12/03/book-trailers-11-steps-to-make-your-own/

Penn, J. (2015). *Book trailers and using video for book marketing*. Retrieved from http://www.thecreativepenn.com/2015/03/02/book-trailers/

Pinto Pires, S. (2010). Give Voicethread to your students! *E-blahblah*. Retrieved from http://e-blahblah.com/index.php/2010/02/give-voicethread-to-your-students

Plickers. (2016). *Tailor instruction with instant feedback*. Retrieved from http://plickers.com

Prapinwong, M., & Puthikanon, N. (2008). An evaluation of an internet-based learning model from EFL perspectives. *Asian EFL Journal, 27*, 1-50.

Prensky, M. (2001). Digital natives, digital immigrants. *On the Horizon, 9*(5). Retrieved from http://www.marcprensky.com/writing/Prensky%20-%20Digital%20Natives,%20Digital%20Immigrants%20-%20Part1.pdf

Poelzer, T. (2009). VoiceThreads in the classroom. Tech it up! *Bringing Technology to the Classroom*. Thompson Rivers University. Kamloops, British Columbia. October 22 – 24, Canada.

Recchio-Demmin, B. (2009). Using VoiceThread as a tool for language learning. *Technology and Collaborative Creativity in Learning (TaCCL) Lab, University at Albany, SUNY*. Retrieved from http://tccl.rit.albany.edu/knilt/index.php/Using_VoiceThread_as_a_Tool_for_Language_Learning

Sambuchino, C. (2016). *How to make a book trailer: 6 steps*. Retrieved from http://www.writersdigest.com/editor-blogs/guide-to-literary-agents/how-to-make-a-book-trailer-6-tips

Schiller, M. (2015). *Spotlight on business: 4 elements of an awesome Animoto book trailer*. Retrieved from https://animoto.com/blog/business/animato-book-trailer/

Smith, J. & Dobson, E. (2009). Beyond the book: Using VoiceThread in language arts instruction. In T. Bastiaens, J. Dron & C. Xin (Eds.), *Proceedings of World Conference on E-Learning in Corporate, Government, Healthcare, and Higher Education 2009* (pp. 712-715). Chesapeake, VA: AACE. Retrieved from http://www.editlib.org/p/32538

Sun, Y., Yu, J. & Gao, F. (2013). Shared video media: A new environment to support peer feedback in second language learning. In R. McBride & M. Searson (Eds.), *Proceedings of Society for Information Technology & Teacher Education International Conference 2013.* (pp. 1746-1751). Chesapeake, VA: AACE.

Tech4Learning, Inc. (2016). *Pics4Learning.* Retrieved from http://pics4learning.com/

Tinto, V. (2003). Learning better together: The impact of learning communities on Student Success. *Higher Education Monograph Series, 1.*

Vesper, S. (2008). Voicethread examples in education. *Slideshare.* Retrieved from http://www.slideshare.net/suziea/voicethread-examples-in-education-presentation#

VoiceThread. (2016). VoiceThread LLC. Retrieved from http://www.voicethread.com

Vygotsky, L. (1978). Interaction between learning and development. *Mind and Society.* Cambridge, MA: Harvard University Press.

WikiHow. (2016). *How to do a presentation in class.* Retrieved from http://www.wikihow.com/Do-a-Presentation-in-Class

Wortham, J. (2007). After 10 years of blogs, the future's brighter than ever. *Wired.* Retrieved from http://archive.wired.com/entertainment/theweb/news/2007/12/blog_anniversary

Yamauchi, M. (2009). Integrating internet technology into EFL classroom: A case study. *International Journal of Pedagogies and Learning, 5*(2), 3.

Yang, S. H. (2009). Using blogs to enhance critical reflection and community of practice. *Journal of Educational Technology & Society, 12*(2), 11-21.

Yang, C., & Chang, Y. S. (2012). Assessing the effects of interactive blogging on student attitudes towards peer interaction, learning motivation, and academic achievements. *Journal of Computer Assisted Learning, 28*(2) 126-135.

Zlatkovska, E. (2010). Webquests as a constructivist tool in the EFL teaching methodology class in a university in Macedonia. *CORELL: Computer Resources for Language Learning 3*, 14-24.

Glossary

BYOD	Bring Your Own Device
CMC	Computer Mediated Communication
EFL	English as a Foreign Language
ESL	English as a Second Language
FAQ	Frequently Asked Questions
HTML	Hypertext Markup Language
LOTE	Languages Other than English
LMS	Learning Management System
PLE	Personal Learning Environment
RSS	Really Simple Syndication
TESOL	Teaching English to Speakers of Other Languages
UGC	User-Generated Content
WYSIWYG	What You See Is What You Get
ZPD	Zone of Proximal Development

About the Book

In a world where there is still a digital divide, and where many second-language learners are digital natives, the internet has unquestionably come to provide significant impact on the way that we communicate, teach, learn, and live. The major pedagogical promise has come with the shift away from the static provision of information to that of dynamic information sharing and user-generated content. The internet has become much more than a source of authentic materials and supplemental resources for the teaching of English to speakers of other languages (TESOL); it now provides a means for students to engage in functional communicative experiences, write and communicate with a wider audience, and showcase their work. All kinds of topics and resources are available, but as most are unsuitable for language learning, they need to be selected wisely. Guidance needs to be effective, and those with little experience in using digital tools and websites for learning need to be kept from becoming disengaged. This is where the teacher and this book perform a critical role.

In this book, the focus is on the use of various tools and techniques that help students to express themselves and to learn with technology, particularly those which rely on the internet to function, those that have been around since the dawn of the internet, and those that have evolved with the growth of the internet. Specifically covered is: world-wide-web utilization for the fostering and development of multiple literacies through socio-constructivist learning via the WebQuest model, constructing visually-based asynchronous digital conversations with VoiceThread, and developing user-generated content with blogs and wikis. The book is intended to be read in whole or in part by teachers, students, parents, and any other stakeholders who may be interested in the topics.

About the Author

David Kent is an Assistant Professor at the Graduate School of TESOL-MALL at Woosong University in the Republic of Korea. He has been working and teaching in Korea since 1995, and with a Doctorate of Education from Curtin University in Australia, he is a specialist in computer assisted language learning (CALL) and the teaching of English to speakers of other languages (TESOL). He has presented at international conferences, as well as published a number of peer-reviewed journal articles, books, and book chapters in his areas of specialization.

Also by David Kent

A Loanword Approach to the Teaching of English as a Foreign Language in Korea:
Exploring the Effectiveness of a Multimedia Curriculum

Teaching with Technology:
Integrating Technology into the TESOL Classroom

Internet in Education:
Integrating the Internet into the TESOL Classroom

TESOL Strategy Guides
Digital Storytelling
The Prezi Presentation Paradigm
Podcasts and Screencasts
WebQuests
VoiceThreading
Blogs and Wikis

www.ingramcontent.com/pod-product-compliance
Lightning Source LLC
Chambersburg PA
CBHW021219090426

42740CB00006B/279